The Malines Conversations

The Beginnings of Anglican-Roman Catholic Dialogue

Rowan Williams

Paulist Press
New York / Mahwah, NJ

Cover image by Bedlovska Liana / Shutterstock.com
Cover design by Joe Gallagher
Book design by Lynn Else

Library of Congress Cataloging-in-Publication Data
Names: Williams, Rowan, 1950– author.
Title: The Malines conversations : the beginnings of Anglican-Roman Catholic dialogue / Rowan Williams.
Description: New York / Mahwah, NJ : Paulist Press, [2021] | Summary: "In 1921, Cardinal Mercier invited a group of visitors from the Roman Catholic Church and the Church of England to his residence to spend a couple of days discussing the issues separating the Anglican and Roman Catholic Churches. This meeting and three that followed, are seen as the precursor to the work of the Anglican-Roman Catholic International Commission (ARCIC), which has been moving this dialogue forward since 1969" —Provided by publisher.
Identifiers: LCCN 2021017042 (print) | LCCN 2021017043 (ebook) | ISBN 9780809155873 (paperback) | ISBN 9781587689895 (ebook)
Subjects: LCSH: Malines Conversations, 1921-1925. | Anglican Communion—Relations—Catholic Church—History. | Catholic Church—Relations—Anglican Communion—History. | Anglican/Roman Catholic International Commission—History.
Classification: LCC BX5004.2 .W55 2021 (print) | LCC BX5004.2 (ebook) | DDC 280/.042—dc23

ISBN 978-0-8091-5587-3 (paperback)
ISBN 978-1-58768-989-5 (e-book)

Published by Paulist Press
997 Macarthur Boulevard
Mahwah, New Jersey 07430
www.paulistpress.com

Printed and bound in the
United States of America

Contents

Foreword

The Malines Conversations represent a unique event in twentieth-century church history. In the 1920s, a number of leading Anglican and Catholic scholars, with the knowledge of their respective Church authorities, entered into dialogue with each other in a climate where this was by no means to be expected. They were discussing a number of crucial issues that made unity between the two communities difficult, such as the Petrine office of the pope and the nature of dogmatic definitions. Many of those themes are still relevant today, especially in the context of ecumenism.

Cardinal Désiré-Joseph Mercier, archbishop of Malines-Brussels from 1906 until his death in 1926, was an enthusiastic supporter of the Malines Conversations. Not only did he show a great personal interest in the matters being discussed, but he also acted as host. Moreover, he had informally consulted Benedict XV, the pope at that time, about this wonderful initiative. The Anglican participants knew they had the support of the archbishops of Canterbury and York.

The contours of the Malines Conversations are skillfully outlined in this publication by Rowan Williams, former archbishop of Canterbury and internationally recognized theologian. He reflects on the ecclesiastical context of the time, on the intellectual profile of the various participants, on the themes that were discussed, and on the meaning of the Conversations for today. We are particularly grateful to him for this *tour de force*, for it is not easy to present the historical and theological complexity of the past in a way we can understand today.

The Malines Conversations are much more than a fascinating episode in the history of ecumenism. They are also more than a welcome glimpse of the striving for unity among Christians at a time that is sometimes mistakenly associated with rigidity or lack of creativity. Perhaps the Malines Conversations may be seen as an example of what is so beautifully called in English *serendipity*. From a set of circumstances and factors, which are in large part accidental, something significant emerges, which, nevertheless, in order to be recognized requires a special openness.

It is for such openness toward the Malines Conversations that I would like to make a plea. They are worth studying, not only from the standpoint of the academic expert, but by anyone concerned for the unity of the Christian Churches. The Malines Conversations are also worth remembering at a deeper and more spiritual level. They are in many ways a source of inspiration to which we can go to refresh ourselves. That is why they deserve to be inscribed more powerfully in our collective memory. We would do well to internalize the "spirit" of the Malines Conversations, using them more frequently as a reference point for meetings of all kinds as well as for our life in the Church. In short, we should cherish them for a variety of reasons.

There is, of course, the link with Mechelen itself, the city, and the archdiocese, and therefore with the Belgian Church province as a whole. We ought to be aware that what took place in the Belgian context was truly a gift to the universal Church. This realization should certainly not give rise to misplaced vanity, but there is nothing wrong in standing with some inevitable pride within the flow of what was conceived and accomplished at the time. This implies a willingness to seize an opportunity when it arises, if by so doing you can take things forward. In other words, it signifies a receptivity to grace, to insight that develops not through mere personal effort and merit but in patient dialogue.

Foreword

The participants of the Malines Conversations knew that they were participating in something exceptional. Above all, they wished for a deep transformation that would bring Christians closer together despite historical divisions and theological barriers. There is no doubt that many people of goodwill can subscribe to this hope today. The dream that Christians can do something real to unite people today is by no means an illusion from a former era. It is a call to which we must all commit ourselves each day.

The Malines Conversations also reveal something important about friendship. Friendship is more than respect, but it cannot exist without it. It is also more than loyalty and faithfulness, and more than mutual feelings of affection. But again, friendship cannot do without these aspects, and can even find excellent expression in them. Friendship is, however, also about personal commitment and belief in the same ideals. In this respect, perhaps even more than in other areas, we can learn from the Malines Conversations. The content of the discussions at that time is sometimes outdated, and the formulations used in the debates certainly are, but what endures is a profound commitment to Christian ecumenism based on personal bonds of friendship. Such a testimony can do much good to both the Church and the world today.

With these final words, then, I can "in friendship" recommend this book to all who share this deep longing, and all those who associate themselves with the continuing prayer of our Lord, "that they may all be one."

Cardinal Jozef De Kesel
Mechelen, February 2, 2021

The Malines Conversations Group

This publication has been produced with the help of the Malines Conversations Group. This is a group of some twenty Anglican and Roman Catholic theologians who have set themselves the goal of reflecting, in the spirit of the original Malines Conversations, on ways of furthering Christian unity between their respective Churches. The group has received the blessing of the respective church authorities—both Anglican and Catholic—and has connections with official bodies such as ARCIC (The Anglican-Roman Catholic International Commission) and IARCCUM (The International Anglican-Roman Catholic Commission on Unity and Mission). However, the group functions informally and independently. This has the great advantage that it can speak freely, even on issues that are very sensitive or controversial in ecumenism.

The Malines Conversations Group has been privileged in its co-patrons. Bishop Rowan Williams, former archbishop of Canterbury, gave the group his full support from the beginning as did Cardinal Godfried Danneels, former archbishop of Mechelen-Brussels, who sadly died in 2019. The group was delighted when his successor as archbishop of Mechelen-Brussels, Cardinal Jozef De Kesel, generously accepted an invitation to be its co-patron.

The Malines Conversations

The Malines Conversations Group wishes to express its warm thanks to its patrons for their encouragement and support, and especially for the texts they have contributed to this publication that celebrates the centenary of the beginning of the Malines Conversations in December 1921.

The group was formed about ten years ago and meets annually for one week, often in a place that has particular resonance for Anglicans and Catholics. In the past, meetings were held in Canterbury, Rome, York, and Boston, among other places. It is no coincidence that the first meeting was held in Belgium. The members of the group, coming from four continents, were welcomed at the Abbey of Chevetogne and of course visited Mechelen, where the table around which the historical conversations took place is kept in the archiepiscopal palace.

When the group meets, it is not only to listen to papers on history and theology, important though these are in the ongoing course of its work. Time together is also about proper opportunities for reflection, alongside discussion, celebration, and, above all, prayer. It is only by getting to know each other thoroughly and in all respects, and by building friendships, that anything can really move. Themes discussed in recent years have included the transforming power of the Word of God, the specificity of the Christian image of humanity, the interpretation of ordination in both traditions, and the meaning of the concept of sacramentality. It is no exaggeration to say that the annual study and discussion weeks are a great enrichment for all participants.

It is precisely for this reason that the Malines Conversations Group aims to share its experience and reflection with as many people as possible. The encounter with the other is always an invitation for the self to reposition and reinterpret itself. No one has ever benefited from an identity that remains unchanging and unchanged. To assume such a position leads to pain, stubbornness, and distortion. The importance of facing one's own vulnerabilities and being sensitive to those of others, on the other hand, is a message that is worth repeating today. The Malines Conversations Group is committed to spreading that message through various initiatives, within and outside the life of the Church, the one Body of Christ.

1

Introduction

In the exceptionally cold December of 1921, Désiré-Joseph Mercier, the cardinal archbishop of Malines (Mechelen),[1] welcomed to his residence a small group of visitors from the Church of England. They were joined by the cardinal's vicar general (and eventual successor), Jozef Van Roey, and a priest of the Lazarist Congregation, Fernand Portal, with a view to spending a couple of days in theological discussion about the issues separating the Anglican and Roman Catholic communions. Three further meetings followed, in March and November 1923 and in May 1925, with several additional participants on both sides. But the deaths of both Mercier and Portal in 1926—as well as the emergence of considerable public controversy over the conversations in both Anglican and Roman Catholic circles—marked a watershed. A brief session in October 1926, under the presidency of Van Roey, agreed on the wording of two formal reports on behalf of the two parties but contributed no substantive new material for discussion. It was clear that the experiment was over.

The Malines Conversations are usually seen as the precursor to the work of the Anglican-Roman Catholic International Commission (ARCIC) in recent decades. Most of us know something about ARCIC, and we tend to take for granted that sustained discussions and cordial relations between Anglicans and

Roman Catholics are a good thing. It is hard now to realize how bold a step was being taken in 1921. But at the same time, while we have come a long way since 1921, it is important to recognize that in some ways the problems discussed at Malines are still with us. Revisiting the Malines process and some of the topics covered in these meetings helps us see how and why certain problem areas in relations between Anglicans and Roman Catholics have remained persistently on the table without ever being satisfactorily resolved, despite the labors of ARCIC and the great intellectual and spiritual resource represented by the statements of that body.

This brief reflection on the Conversations does not attempt to give a detailed history of the meetings (there are several excellent and accessible accounts, beginning with the recollections of some of the participants themselves[2]), but rather to look at some of the interests of those directly involved, at the background concerns that shaped the meetings, and, most importantly, at the unresolved questions identified in the sessions and still overshadowing the search for unity between the Anglican and Roman Catholic communions in our own day. And, as will become clear, some at least of these have implications for a much wider ecumenical and theological agenda.

Most of the specific points at issue in the Malines discussions relate to two basic concerns. First, what is the proper relation between the Church of God in one particular place and the Church of God in every place—the Church as the one Body of Christ extended in time and space? Second, obviously related to this first point, what exactly does it mean to recognize the *same* faith in diverse communities, communities separated by language and culture, by different historical trajectories and social circumstances? Some of the most significant contributions to the Malines discussions focus on these problems. The way they are addressed is, as we shall see, very much affected by the theological climate of the age, and most modern readers will sometimes feel a little puzzled as to why this or that specific issue is given prominence, or why certain theological first principles are not drawn out as clearly as they might have been; but it is undeniable that in their day the Malines debates broke new ground, not least in the way they were conducted—respectful, enquiring, careful to understand the weight of another's point of view. They laid foundations for a quite new kind of discussion between separated Christian bodies about the theology of the Church. And today, as the various Christian confessions become more aware—sometimes painfully aware—of the challenges of being recognizable to each other across cultural divisions, it may be that reflection on the Malines experience will bring some light on crucial matters of shared Christian concern.

Personalities

The Malines Conversations would not have taken place had it not been for the friendship between two unusual and very different people—an English aristocrat and a French priest of humble origins. **Charles Lindley Wood, second Viscount Halifax** (1839–1934), was an active layman of the Church of England. He was on close and friendly terms with its leaders but was also deeply committed to the cause of those in the Church of England who were working to bring its liturgy and spirituality into fuller accord with Catholic practice—a minority within the established Church, but an increasingly vocal one. Halifax had been president since 1868 of the English Church Union, a body founded to defend and promote the Anglo-Catholic view of the Church of England. This view had developed in contrast to that of Anglican evangelicals who tended to view the national Church as essentially a local Protestant body, and also to the older "High Church" party, who, in spite of a strong tradition of sacramental theology, had defended the legal establishment of the Church as a necessary aspect of a "confessional" state ruled by a legitimate Christian monarch presiding over the Church's counsels. Anglo-Catholics strongly resisted the idea that the state should have authority in matters of worship and theology and insisted on the need to restore relations with—and a measure of conformity to—the wider Catholic body of Western Christendom. Throughout his long life, Halifax campaigned for these concerns, winning affection and respect even from convinced opponents because of his manifest spiritual integrity and personal generosity.

Étienne Fernand Portal (1855–1926) was a member of the Congregation of the Mission (otherwise known as Lazarists or Vincentians after their founder, St. Vincent de Paul) who spent much of his ministry as a seminary professor (his health prevented him working abroad as a missionary). He was in touch and in sympathy with figures like the formidable Louis Duchesne (1843–1922), the greatest ecclesiastical historian of his era in France and one of the foremost in Europe, a man wholly committed to guaranteeing that the best of historical and critical scholarship should find a home in the Catholic Church. He also developed an active interest in the theology of Russian Orthodoxy. In the early 1890s, he was studying the provocative essays of the great Russian thinker Aleksei Stepanovich Khomyakov (published in 1872 as *L'Église Latine et le Protestantisme*), in which he would have found an articulate critique of centralism and authoritarianism in the Church, and a powerful advocacy for the idea of a Church defined less by authoritative statements and directive government and more by the "catholic" quality of its life, its commitment to shared discernment and mutual service. Khomyakov believed that both Latin Catholicism and Protestantism failed to understand this: they were simply two sides of a coin, neither of them able to grasp the basic nature of the Church's communal reality (*sobornost* in Khomyakov's terminology, from the Slavonic adjective *soborny*, which had been used to translate the Greek *katholike* in the liturgical Slavonic version of the Nicene Creed).

He saw Latin Catholicism maintaining a system of top-down hierarchical control and Protestantism rebelling in the name of individual liberty, with neither side really attending to what was unique about the experience of the Church as a body in which real mutual communion was realized, a genuine release from individualism and rivalry, but also from authoritarian control and the passion for conformity.[3] Along with many of his friends and interlocutors, Portal was to face discipline for his supposed sympathies with Modernism, at a time when any defense of disinterested scholarly method in scriptural study or doctrinal history was liable to provoke such accusations.

Halifax and Portal met in Madeira in 1890 (Portal was visiting for the sake of his health, as was Halifax's son, who was suffering from tuberculosis). They became lifelong and intimate friends; Halifax was able to explain to Portal some of his experience of and hopes for the Church of England, and Portal became convinced of the need for Roman Catholics, especially in France, to hear more of the "Catholic Revival" in the Church of England. With Halifax's support, he founded in 1895 a weekly journal with this aim, the *Revue Anglo-Romaine*, which published a variety of articles on historical and theological topics until its suppression in 1896. In the minds of both Halifax and Portal, this enterprise was closely connected with an attempt to secure from Rome a recognition that Anglicans possessed true priestly Orders. Pope Leo XIII had made friendly overtures to the Eastern Orthodox Churches in the early 1890s, and Portal was encouraged to believe that there was the possibility of a more flexible attitude toward the Church of England as well. He published (under a pseudonym) a pamphlet examining the case for the recognition of Anglican Orders and apparently concluding for their invalidity, but on grounds so slender and so historically shaky that a discerning reader might well have thought that the piece was designed as a provocation. If so, it succeeded to the extent that the historian Louis Duchesne wrote an article declaring in favor of validity. But the result of the pressure to examine the case for Anglican Orders was the papal declaration of September 1896, *Apostolicae curae*, with its well-known negative verdict on the validity of the Anglican ordination rite. It is fairly clear from what Portal later wrote that his hope had never been for a full-scale official investigation but for a more detached discussion of the theological issues, a discussion that would involve Anglican and Roman Catholic scholars together.[4] But in the light of the formal declaration, it was in effect impossible to proceed with any such discussion at this point; the *Revue*, which briefly attempted to argue that the Roman decision was not irrevocable, was the subject of severe censure from Rome, and the archbishop of Paris demanded its suppression. Portal complied.

But it is not difficult to see that the Malines enterprise was an attempt to take forward what had been frustrated in the 1890s—the hope for a careful and well-resourced discussion, not dominated by the need to come to any final determination. Portal never abandoned his conviction that Roman Catholics on the continent of Europe had a narrow and inadequate picture of Anglican identity, past and present, and was more than ready to cooperate again with Halifax when a window of opportunity presented itself. This took the shape of the "Appeal to All Christian People" issued by the Anglican Lambeth Conference of 1920. This was the first gathering after the First World War of Anglican bishops from around the world, and the participants in the Conference were very conscious both of the sense of urgency around reconciliation and united Christian witness that was widely felt in the wake of the terrible carnage of the war, and also, to a lesser extent, of the need for more knowledge of and support for the various Eastern Christian communities, from the Armenians and Assyrians of the Middle East, who had suffered appalling persecution in recent decades, to the Russians now living under an openly atheistic regime. **Randall Davidson** (1848–1930), archbishop of Canterbury from 1903 to 1928, had been an eloquent advocate for these communities during and after the war, and relations with Eastern Christians were warm at this period.[5] It would have seemed reasonable to assume that Davidson would be broadly in sympathy with a friendly approach to the great Communion of Western Christendom in the search for Christian reconciliation and joint witness. When approached informally by Halifax about the plans for conversations, the archbishop was hesitant and initially unwilling to give any hint of official status to the conversations, either by proposing possible participants or by vetoing names suggested by Halifax. Naturally, he wanted assurances from the Roman Catholic side that they too were acting with some degree of formal approval before he would be willing to give any impression of formal endorsement by nominating spokesmen. But, once that assurance had been given, he defended the process and was prepared to make suggestions regarding Anglican members of the group.[6]

Essentially, what the Lambeth statement of 1920 set out was the vision of a journey toward a unity that would not involve the unilateral submission of any one Christian community to another's discipline, but a reciprocal reconciliation of ministries, based on Scripture, the Catholic Creeds, and the two sacraments instituted by Christ. The idea of a universal episcopate is presented as the only effective and credible vehicle "for maintaining the unity and coherence of the Church,"[7] but the Lambeth bishops affirm their willingness "to accept from these authorities [i.e., of other communions]" any "form of commission or recognition which would commend our ministry to their congregations"[8] — in the hope that the ministers of other communions would do the same. A good many took this to imply that Anglicans would under certain circumstances submit to some kind of conditional reordination by Roman Catholic or Eastern Orthodox hierarchs; but equally the plain meaning of the words is that they would accept some kind of public commissioning from non-Anglican Protestant bodies.

For its period it is an astonishingly bold proposal; and it is easy to see how someone like Portal could seize on this as an occasion for reopening the question about Anglican Orders from a new point of view—not directly challenging the conclusions of *Apostolicae curae* but identifying a practical way of moving toward corporate reunion and a unified ministry, unified at least in the sense that it was universally recognized. Although some, like the eloquent and combative bishop of Durham, Herbert Hensley Henson, could dismiss such a vision as a compound of sentimentality toward Eastern Christians and a continuing inflexibility about nonepiscopal confessions in the United Kingdom,[9] it is more than that, to the degree that it acknowledges not only the "spiritual reality" of nonepiscopal ministry, but the need to *receive* some kind of ministerial grace at the hands of that ministry. And in apparently allowing the possibility of some sacramental confirmatory rite to be received from Catholic or Orthodox colleagues, it suggests a dramatic way of breaking the deadlock over "validity."

The degree to which Davidson himself was personally completely supportive of this is somewhat uncertain; it is unlikely that he believed the Lambeth proposal would have any immediate effect. But whatever his views, by the mid-1920s he was embroiled in a bitter internal controversy in the Church of England that made any thoughts of conditional reordination an unfeasibly remote idea. Decades of ill-tempered and badly managed efforts to secure a measure of liturgical conformity in the Church of England (largely directed against Anglo-Catholic innovations or—as they would have seen them—revivals in liturgical practice) had finally issued in proposals for a revision of the *Book of Common Prayer*, allowing a little more flexibility in worship, presenting a new rite for the Eucharist, slightly adapted in a "Catholic" direction, and permitting the reservation of the Eucharistic elements for exclusively pastoral purposes (communion for the sick and dying). These revisions, while seen as inadequate by most Anglo-Catholics, especially those closest to Halifax himself, were greeted with something like paranoia in more Protestant quarters, where they were represented as a surrender to papal doctrine. Davidson came under intense pressure over this and was not eager to appear in public as supporting anything that could give further offence by implying concessions to Roman Catholic authority. His cautious initial support for Malines, and his continuing quiet encouragement (both, in fact, courageous in the circumstances) had to be balanced by the need to reassure anxious Protestants that no formal "negotiation" was under way; and he took to heart the risk that an Anglican delegation composed entirely of Lord Halifax's nominees might give a somewhat slanted picture of the Church of England.

One factor that undoubtedly affected Davidson's response and helped overcome any hesitations was the stature of the proposed host for the conversations, **Désiré-Joseph Mercier** (1851–1926), archbishop of Malines since 1905. Mercier was by 1921 a figure with a global reputation, thanks to his outspokenly courageous mobilization of the Belgian Church's resources in resisting the German invasion and occupation during the First World War. He had already, before becoming a bishop, been a leading figure in the revival of Thomist philosophy at the University of Louvain/Leuven and had worked hard to protect serious scholars from the charge of Modernism. He never accepted the facile disjunction that was enshrined in many Catholic circles at the time between "Modernist" historical study and the supposedly timeless truths of scholastic thought—a fact that must have predisposed him to be sympathetic to some styles of Anglican theology. In the immediate postwar period, he had also traveled widely in the United States to raise money for the restoration of the University Library at Louvain (destroyed during the German invasion). During these travels, he had met with several non-Roman Catholic church leaders (including bishops of the Protestant Episcopal Church, the Church of England's sister body in the United States), and his generous references to them as fellow-Christians, "brothers," and colleagues had been denounced to Rome as indicating doctoral indifferentism.[10] He was in every respect a natural figurehead for the Malines project, learned, independent, and widely respected internationally. He faced a difficult task in navigating the Conversations through the stormy waters of Vatican suspicions and negative reactions from Roman Catholics in England but demonstrated complete commitment to the project from beginning to end. One of the most controversial and revolutionary interventions in the Conversations was the result of a direct personal initiative on his part. While he was scrupulous in making it clear that no official or institutional outcomes for the Conversations could be guaranteed, he evidently hoped for some institutional movement in the further future that would actually reconcile the separated bodies.

Like Davidson, he stressed—for the benefit of the authorities in Rome—that the meetings were not strictly meetings of "delegates" or official representatives; no one taking part had a mandate from the highest authorities to engage in any kind of negotiations, and no one could claim to be speaking on behalf of their own Church as a whole. It was a point that Davidson too had to clarify repeatedly, in the face of fierce criticism from British Protestants of all varieties, and of some highly misleading reporting in the British press. But it is significant that, after the second of the meetings, Davidson, concerned by the apparently radical suggestions discussed at the second set of sessions and by hostile responses from some senior figures in the Church of England, took the initiative in nominating two extra Anglican members for the group and in organizing what we should now call a briefing for the group a month before the Conversations were due to happen, a briefing in which several other Anglican scholars of diverse views were involved. Two further members were also added to the Roman Catholic contingent. It is not clear whether the two names were directly sanctioned by Rome; the pope's Secretary of State, Cardinal Gasparri, had in April 1922 expressed the pope's friendly interest and his encouragement for the Conversations, but it is likely that Mercier himself selected the new members. The idea that a voice from the Orthodox Churches might be added was briefly raised by Portal and then abandoned; similarly, the possibility of representation from outside France and Belgium, perhaps even from among British Roman Catholics, was considered but not pursued.

It was not difficult for critics of Malines to argue that neither group could be taken as typical spokesmen for their Church. But it is important to remember that neither Portal nor Halifax was looking for anything resembling a decision-making process. (They had had their fingers burned in the 1890s when their attempts to have the question of Anglican Orders reviewed theologically led to an unwelcome official outcome.) It was reasonable that those involved in the meetings, perhaps especially on the Anglican side, should be those for whom the matters under discussion were of serious theological concern, and who had the kind of scholarly background that allowed them to debate these matters with professional expertise. Bishop Hensley Henson of Durham, a controversialist well known for acidic and uncompromising views, and for a deeply unsympathetic attitude toward Anglo-Catholics, wrote in his journal for January 1923, when Davidson had informed the other English bishops about the Conversations, that he had told the archbishop that the members of the group "were not competent to speak for Anglicanism," since two of them were committed Anglo-Catholics already in substantial agreement with Rome and the third was "a very cryptic type of Anglican."[11] Similarly, when the new members of the group were announced later in the same year, he repeated the same opinion in his journal and wrote a strongly worded letter of protest to the *Times*.

Henson's language both private and public (he uses the word *negotiations*) certainly suggests that he had not registered the point that the Malines Conversations were exploratory and informal;

but he is also less than fair to at least some of the participants. The "very cryptic type of Anglican" mentioned in the journal was the dean of Wells Cathedral (and former dean of Westminster), **Joseph Armitage Robinson** (1858–1933), a patristic scholar and medievalist of enormous international reputation. He was indeed difficult to place in the geography of Anglican party conflicts: he had grown up in a distinctly evangelical environment and then absorbed the theology of the great biblical theologians of Cambridge in the later nineteenth century—Westcott, Lightfoot, and Hort—with their vision of Christ as restoring universal human community and cosmic harmony. He moved toward an Anglo-Catholic position in some—but decidedly not all—respects (his theology of the eucharist, e.g., was definitely in the Calvinist tradition and not at all sympathetic to the robust affirmation of an objective sacramental presence that could be the object of adoration), and his scholarship proved helpful to Anglo-Catholic critics of the proposed new prayer book. At Malines, he was to present a lucid survey of the New Testament evidence for a distinctive Petrine calling or charism, and the records of the actual conversations, as well as his own written recollections, make it clear that he was prepared to countenance a heavily modified theology of Petrine ministry, with no jurisdictional elements. Whatever Henson's view, he was in no sense what some in those years called an "Anglo-Papalist."[12]

Walter Howard Frere (1863–1938) was undoubtedly closer to Halifax; but his background as cofounder and Superior of the Community of the Resurrection, an Anglican religious order with an ethos somewhere between Benedictine and Dominican, and his reputation as an expert in medieval liturgy meant that he was familiar with a larger world than that of the Anglo-Catholic parishes with their struggles for freedom to restore a full Latinate ritual. He also took a strong scholarly interest in the history of the Russian Church. His support for the revised prayer book was to make him somewhat suspect in the strictest Anglo-Catholic circles; and his appointment in 1923 as bishop of Truro placed him in an awkward but important position, as an interpreter to the bishops of the hopes and anxieties of the Anglo-Catholics and an informal channel of communication for the bishops to that constituency. The records of the discussions show that Frere, although he did not himself present any papers of his own to the group, entirely shared Robinson's attitude to the Petrine ministry and was willing to articulate this strongly. He also offered, early in the discussions, his own reading of the "Appeal to All Christian People," claiming—rather optimistically—that Anglican bishops would have no difficulty in accepting a sacramental regularizing of their position in the event of full theological reconciliation being agreed.

Davidson's extra nominees in 1923 were **Charles Gore** (1853–1932), who had been bishop of Oxford until 1919, and **Beresford James Kidd** (1864–1948), warden of Keble College, Oxford—both indisputably identified with Anglo-Catholicism, but both, like Frere, at some distance from Halifax's almost unbroken optimism about the possibilities of reconciliation and less committed than Halifax to the more vocal and uncompromising elements in the Anglo-Catholic party. Indeed, Gore had been one of those who protested to Davidson at the report of the second of the Conversations. He had duly paid the price commonly paid by intelligent critics who are immediately recruited to improve the balance of a group. Gore had been the main inspiration for the foundation of the Community of the Resurrection, and he had also been a hugely influential voice in advocating for the acceptance by orthodox Anglo-Catholics of some aspects of historical-critical scholarship. A convinced Christian Socialist, his attitudes would have resonated with Portal's enthusiasm for the social teaching of Leo XIII, though we have no evidence that the two men discussed these subjects. Like Frere, his role as an episcopal spokesman for the "Catholic" position brought him some measure of suspicion from both bishops and Anglo-Catholics. It is clear that his participation in the Malines discussions was forceful and independent, to a degree that caused Halifax some anxiety, but his views were quite clearly supported by both Robinson and Frere. A very full statement of his difficulties with the Roman system at the fourth meeting, which prompted an equally full and careful response from one of the Roman Catholic participants, was evidently seen by some of the Anglicans (not least Halifax, who was anxious about so explicitly critical an intervention) as a crucial "line in the sand," although it was also welcomed by the non-Anglican participants for its clarity and energy.

Kidd was, like Robinson, a patristic scholar, though not of comparable international standing, and he also had an interest in some of the questions around history and canon law that were in the background of the Conversations. A little closer to Halifax than any of the other Anglican participants, one of his major contributions was a fairly brief but sophisticated essay dealing with the different ways in which papal authority had been seen theologically and legally in pre-Reformation England, with the aim of clarifying exactly what the English Reformers thought they were denying in refusing papal jurisdiction. Kidd was, in fact, echoing aspects of a particular tradition of Anglo-Catholic apologetic that had some popularity in the early decades of the twentieth century. This involved arguing that the sixteenth century reforms of the English Church had been imposed by the state and had on the whole not been initiated or even endorsed by the Church's own organs of governance, so that the Church itself could not be held guilty of deliberate schism or the explicit rejection of the discipline of the Western Church. The two provinces of Canterbury and York had in effect been forcibly severed from the rest of the Western Church by an illegitimate exercise of royal authority. Kidd does not present this (historically shaky) case in its full detail, and he would certainly not have agreed with it without reservation; but his analysis of how papal authority was understood allows him to argue that for the Church of England *now* to recognize some form of Petrine ministry and spiritual authority is in no way a betrayal of the Reformation's rejection of the disproportionate claims made for the papacy in medieval and modern times.

The truth is that despite the complaints about the unrepresentative nature of the Anglican party at Malines, none of the members of the group could be seen as uncritical in respect of the contemporary Roman Catholic system, and most were not afraid to be explicit about their criticisms. They were fortunate in having Roman Catholic respondents who could register their concerns with sympathy and do more than simply rehearse standard official arguments. **Jozef-Ernest Van Roey** (1874–1961) shared many of Mercier's interests and, like him, had a distinguished academic record at Louvain; like Mercier, he was also much influenced by the Irish Benedictine spiritual writer Columba Marmion, who spent most of his life in Belgian monasteries and whose theological teaching exhibits a rich interweaving of doctrinal and spiritual themes. His interventions in the discussions at Malines were mostly directed at questions to do with the pope's jurisdiction, and he presented a paper at the fourth Conversation giving a theological perspective on the pope's relations with the episcopate, a topic raised several times during the meetings.

The two Roman Catholic "latecomers" to the Conversations, introduced at the same point at which Gore and Kidd joined the Anglican side, were both distinguished ecclesiastical historians. **Pierre Batiffol** (1861–1929) had been head of the Institut Catholique at Toulouse and was the founder of the *Revue Biblique* (along with Marie-Joseph Lagrange), which aimed at introducing a French Catholic public to biblical criticism, as well as of the *Revue de littérature ecclésiastique*. His selection by Mercier as a member of the group seems, from a contemporary perspective, somewhat provocative: he had been dismissed from his position at the Institut Catholique as a suspected Modernist, and, like Duchesne, had been heavily criticized for bringing ordinary critical methods to bear on the history of the Church and even the history of doctrine. Yet he was evidently regarded as a good match for Robinson (whom he already knew) in terms of sheer technical scholarly proficiency; it was he who was deputed to reply to Robinson's essay on the Petrine ministry at the third Conversation, which he did at length (twenty pages in the published version), working through all Robinson's examples, as well as to Kidd's paper on the patristic exegesis of these passages. At the fourth meeting, he had the equally demanding task of replying to Bishop Gore's paper on the limits of doctrinal diversity. It would be fair to say that in the third and fourth sets of sessions at Malines, Batiffol was the dominant theological voice on the Roman Catholic side. But **Hippolyte Hemmer** (1864–1945), a French parish priest who had taught at the Institut Catholique in Paris and was a noted expert on the apostolic fathers, provided further solid patristic expertise, especially on questions to do with the development of the Petrine ministry. He contributed a paper on this topic at the fourth set of sessions, and the record shows that he elaborated on this *librement* in his oral presentation and that he noted the potential of Anglican theory and practice in encouraging a less centralized approach to authority in the Catholic Church, while also, in a later session, observing the difficulties posed for Roman Catholics by the variety of doctrinal positions tolerated in the Church of England.

One other name must be mentioned, although he was not himself present at the Conversations: **Dom Lambert Beauduin** (1873–1960) was at that time a monk of the Abbey of Mont-César in Louvain and a professor at the Benedictine college of Sant' Anselmo in Rome. Mercier had known him for some time and had been impressed by his ecumenical enthusiasm and his commitment to liturgical reform. He was to become especially well known as the founder of a new Benedictine community, first at Amay-sur-Meuse, later at Chevetogne, in which both Eastern and Western liturgical practices were followed, and dialogue between separate Christian bodies was seen as the heart of the community's ministry. Mercier commissioned Beauduin to write for the fourth series of sessions in 1925 a paper on a possible new model for corporate reunion; Beauduin produced his now celebrated essay *L'Église anglicaine réunie non absorbée*, which Mercier read (without naming its author) to a somewhat startled gathering at the third session on May 20.[13] Mercier himself was obviously attracted by the model outlined, but the other non-Anglican participants were less impressed (Batiffol described Beauduin's ideas as *pleine utopie*). The Anglicans seem to have been equally taken aback at this proposal, which envisaged a "patriarchate" of Canterbury comparable to the arrangements made for those groups from the Eastern Churches that had accepted canonical reunion with Rome since the seventeenth century, and Bishop Gore noted that this could hardly be discussed without reference to the bishops of the wider Anglican communion (a rather rare recognition that the issues discussed at Malines affected others than merely English Anglicans). Fuller debate was not easy, as the text of Beauduin's memorandum was not distributed (and indeed was not included with the other material in the agreed report published in 1927). When it was published by Halifax in the personal collection of material that he edited in 1930—without the consent of his coparticipants—it was as controversial as anyone might have expected. But it gives a flavor of the hopes of some at least of the Malines group, and indisputably builds on the themes raised in the first two conversations. For all its glaring flaws as a historical essay, it contributed to the wider ecumenical scene a vivid and compelling picture of an alternative model to that of mere "submission" to the See of Rome. Of all the texts discussed at Malines, it is probably the one that has had the greatest influence in the long run—ironically, since it was not written by a participant.

2

Context

As will be clear by now, the Malines Conversations were regularly overshadowed on the Roman Catholic side by the specter of "Modernism." The term is famously difficult to define, but it was used, especially from the beginning of the twentieth century, to designate a spectrum of scholarly opinion for which both scriptural texts and the history of doctrinal formulation should be seen as subject to the ordinary processes of human intellectual and imaginative development. In plainer terms, this meant that pretty well any attempt to trace the history of a scriptural text or a practice or teaching in the Church according to the sort of methods that would be used in other humanistic disciplines could be seen as "Modernist." Pope Leo XIII had, in the last decade of the nineteenth century, given some limited encouragement to Catholic biblical scholarship, on the grounds that rationalist attacks on the truth of Scripture could be effectively countered only by a more professionally sophisticated level of learning among Catholics; but it proved difficult to decide the point at which this new professionalism had to step back from certain questions because they touched on unchallengeable doctrinal matters. The conclusion (commonplace in non-Catholic scholarship by the 1890s) that Moses could not have been literally the author of the first five books of the Bible was one such issue, partly because Jesus is represented in the Gospels as apparently identifying Moses in these terms. The early days of the *Revue Biblique*, mentioned above, had some difficult moments. Likewise, critical historians such as Duchesne came under suspicion and censure for questioning the veracity of traditional saints' lives, and for writing about the Church's history in terms that gave full weight to ordinary human motivation and to the uncertainties and ambiguities of human decision-making. Earlier in the nineteenth century, some Catholic scholars in Germany had laid the foundations of something like a critical history of doctrine, taking it for granted that formulations changed over the years and that there was a need to sift essential from inessential elements in this story. The great Ignaz von Döllinger (1799–1890) had contributed substantially to this kind of critical doctrinal history in mid-century, but he had also emerged as the leading intellectual presence in the European opposition to the 1870 declaration of papal infallibility and had ended his days under sentence of excommunication. His (guarded) involvement with the "Old Catholic" movement and with brokering doctrinal accord between noninfallibilist Catholics, Anglicans, and Eastern Orthodox meant that he was to be, for the generation that followed, both a seminal and a controversial figure.[1] The piquant fact that he had convened a meeting of liberal Catholic scholars at Malines in 1863 is unlikely to have escaped notice among those suspicious of Mercier's initiative.

It was largely from this intellectual environment that those Catholics came who were sympathetic to reviewing the position on Anglican Orders. The revived and much strengthened scholastic theology that had also been promoted by Leo XIII found it difficult to approach any doctrinal question in a way that allowed for prolonged periods of unclarity and gradual discernment (which is why Newman's theory of development was not popular in "official" Catholic theological circles—and was also embraced by some more liberal thinkers with more enthusiasm than understanding[2]). The case for reexamining Anglican Orders assumed that the Anglican rejection of aspects of a late medieval spirituality and culture of priestly identity and power might not, after all, amount to the wholesale rejection of a classically orthodox doctrine of priestly ministry; and in making such an assumption, it also in effect assumed that theological discourse had a history, and that a responsible contemporary theologian would need to approach this history with some discrimination. It would be important to understand both what Anglicans thought they were rejecting *and* what Roman Catholics thought they were condemning in turn. If both rejection and condemnation could be shown to be in important aspects misdirected, there would obviously be a case for reconsidering both. But this would imply that earlier judgments on the subject had been vulnerable to error or misunderstanding; and this, in the minds of more traditionally minded Catholics, would in turn mean that other doctrinal determinations would be rendered uncertain, and the clarity and consistency of dogma would be undermined. "Modernism" was believed to be fundamentally relativistic, and there were those among liberal Catholic scholars who gave some plausibility to this charge—writers like Alfred Loisy (excommunicated in 1908), who came to see the history of doctrine as a continuum of religious practice and speculation with no clear historically identifiable "core" and no absolute norms to which appeal might be made.

The debate over Anglican Orders, then, was already a tacit one about the limits of historical theology as a critical discipline. In the event, the outcome of this debate in the 1890s was decided on the grounds of the supposed inadequacy of the Anglican Ordinal's wording, and of the earlier judgment on the subject (whose documentation emerged only during the Vatican discussions in the 1890s[3]) given late in the reign of Queen Mary Tudor. Duchesne's favorable view of the Anglican position was very much what might have been expected from an ecclesiastical historian formed in the liberal Catholic mold; Portal's perspective was the same. Even Mercier, whose credentials as a Thomist were beyond reproach, had defended some of the Louvain faculty who had been charged with Modernist tendencies and was not sympathetic to the anti-Modernist zealotry that flourished during the papacy of Pius X. In the event, the Malines Conversations were something of a swan song for this style of critical ecclesiastical history. The fact that they were not pursued at a more formal or institutional level until the later part of the century was not the result simply of the hostility of English Roman Catholics, significant as that was at the time, but of the persisting suspicion of scholars prepared to approach doctrine and discipline with a limited but real recognition of the role of contextual and contingent factors in their evolution.

The Church of England had experienced some comparable tensions, although not at the same level of intensity. Critical historical scholarship had been increasingly accepted as a legitimate part of theological study, and figures like B. F. Westcott and J. B. Lightfoot had in the later nineteenth century helped to dispel any assumption that close study of Scripture and the early Church using the best available critical methods was necessarily an enemy to orthodox faith or Catholic discipline and ecclesiology. Charles Gore had in 1889 edited a volume of essays (*Lux Mundi: A Series of Studies in the Religion of the Incarnation*) by theologians identified with the more Catholic party in the Church of England, which embraced the role of critical biblical scholarship and a measure of doctrinal clarification and simplification in some areas, while insisting firmly on credal orthodoxy. It provoked some hostility among more traditional Anglo-Catholics, who were as inflexible about scriptural inerrancy as their evangelical counterparts and saw critical scholarship as ignoring or belittling the tradition of spiritual and symbolic exegesis. When a group of younger Oxford theologians produced a further book of essays in 1912 under the title *Foundations: A Statement of Christian Belief in Terms of Modern Thought*, some saw this as evidence that the acceptance of critical scholarship led inexorably toward doctrinal indifferentism or relativism: the work was fiercely criticized by another younger scholar, Ronald Knox (who later became a Roman Catholic), who had links to Halifax and was an eloquent exponent of the "Anglo-Papalist" position. However, it would be broadly true to say that Anglo-Catholic theology tended to follow Gore, avoiding both the evangelical commitment to full-blown biblical literalism and the *Foundations* style of mild credal revisionism: the Gospels were not to be seen as vulnerable to critical deconstruction in the way that Old Testament texts might be, and the fundamental doctrines of incarnation and trinity were unambiguously affirmed. As we shall see later, this general approach was what shaped Gore's response to Malines; but in fact, it was representative of a good many Anglicans at the time and could be said to be more or less common ground among the Anglican participants at the Conversations.

In other words, while the Roman Catholic participants will have been conscious of the challenges to their credibility from anti-Modernist quarters, this kind of theological criticism was not an issue on the Anglican side. As should by now be clear, the question of how "representative" the participants in both groups were is a complex one; and there is a good case for saying that the Anglicans were in fact rather more and the Roman Catholics rather less representative than critics at the time — certainly in England — tended to assume. The contextual factor that was more challenging for the Anglicans was far more to do with the perception of Anglo-Catholicism as a source of "lawlessness": Anglo-Catholics had increasingly taken the initiative in adapting the Anglican liturgy in ways that brought it closer to post-Reformation Roman Catholic practice and even wording, using the approved Roman ceremonial and sometimes incorporating texts from the Roman Mass. Despite ingenious attempts to argue that this was not only a legitimate adjustment to pastoral needs but a recognition of the continuing obligation of the Church of England to Catholic canon law, it could only appear to the average British citizen as a refusal to abide by the legally sanctioned forms of Anglican worship. By the first decade of the twentieth century, however, ill-judged attempts to enforce these forms (leading to the imprisonment of a small number of recalcitrant parish clergy) had failed to secure conformity of usage. Proposals for a new *Book of Common Prayer* making some very limited concessions to the Anglo-Catholic agenda were being developed in the period leading up to the First World War, after a Royal Commission had recommended in 1905 that steps might be taken to accommodate some Anglo-Catholic demands to produce a more homogenous and well-regulated liturgical life in the Church of England. At the time when the first Malines Conversations were taking place, these proposals were being finalized for discussion by the newly empowered Church Assembly, a deliberative body of clergy and laity recently set up by Parliament for the preparation and scrutiny of legislation affecting the Church of England.

Archbishop Davidson had been under constant pressure since the first days of his tenure at Canterbury to outlaw Catholicizing changes in the Anglican liturgy, and in the early 1920s, when specific revisions were being debated, that pressure was especially strong. The issue, however, was not simply that of liturgical conformity; the question was to become inextricably bound up with the whole legal position of the Church of England. Davidson had already expressed his unease about Parliament having the last word on liturgical questions, and the final debates on the Revised Prayer Book in 1927 and 1928 show that his misgivings were amply justified. Populist Protestant agitation—some stirred up by politicians who were not themselves members of the Church of England—secured the defeat of the proposals on two separate occasions. It was always going to be a difficult business to persuade a political audience not generally interested in liturgical reform that the suggested changes were worthwhile; but this also meant that agitators against the new liturgy could appeal to one of the strongest surviving popular prejudices among English Christians: the visceral suspicion and hatred of Roman

24

Catholicism. Davidson and nearly all the bishops, as well as most delegates in the Church Assembly, argued in vain against this fixed hostility, but their opponents could not see in the revisions anything but a capitulation to "popery." As Davidson observed in a note of 1928,[4] the logic of these opponents would have been the expulsion from the Church of England of a substantial body of generally loyal and pastorally effective clergy; but the determination of opponents of the new Prayer Book to enforce their views by parliamentary authority also strengthened the hand of those who believed that the legal establishment of the Church of England was an anachronism and worse—a spiritual anomaly, subjecting the Church to an alien secular power. This picture of a Church slavishly compliant to the state was a commonplace in anti-Anglican polemic, not least among English Roman Catholics, and it was not only Anglo-Catholics who were eager to prove its falsity. The Prayer Book debacle did nothing for the credibility of the Establishment of the Church of England, and the rejection of the revisions in 1928 prompted the bishops to the radical step of declaring that they would permit the new texts to be used in the parishes despite being technically illegal.[5]

The point for our purpose is that the Prayer Book revision process was already, by the beginning of the 1920s, threatening the future stability of the Church and the defensibility and coherence of its legal status. As the temperature rose regarding liturgical revision, it was easy enough for any sympathetic engagement with the Roman Catholic Church to be represented as further evidence of the betrayal of the Reformation by the leadership of the English Church, or even of a conspiracy against the Protestant political and religious settlement of the sixteenth century. Davidson's extreme caution about sanctioning the Malines Conversations, about suggesting themes for discussion, and even initially about suggesting members for the Anglican group; his reluctance to make any public announcement concerning the Conversations; and his unwillingness in correspondence with Mercier to commit himself to any clear endorsement of the theological direction of the discussions was interpreted by Mercier as disappointingly chilly. But, as we have seen, Davidson faithfully supported the Conversations and took the (rather risky) initiative of himself announcing their existence and reporting on their progress in a letter to the archbishops of the Anglican communion at Christmas 1923, followed up by a speech to the bishops of the Church of England in February 1924. More than this he could hardly have done without greatly intensifying the anxiety and ill feeling that surrounded the internal debates of the Church of England at the time.

What conclusions can we draw from these considerations of the wider context of the Conversations in both Anglican and Roman Catholic circles? Given the acute tensions around Modernism in the Roman Catholic Church and the intense suspicion of "Romanizing" movements in the Church of England and English society more widely, it seems something of a miracle that the Conversations happened at all. Both Mercier and Davidson were putting their reputations at risk by supporting, even informally, a set of encounters with no clearly envisaged outcome, which also posed fundamental questions to the self-understanding of large parts of their own church communities. It is true that both could have argued that there was potential gain to those communities in the Conversations. There is certainly evidence that Pope Leo XIII was eager to facilitate the return of the English nation to communion with the Holy See.[6] We can easily forget that Great Britain in the last years of the nineteenth century was a major global power; a reconciliation with the main body of English Christians would have been, politically and symbolically, a substantial achievement. The condemnation of Anglican Orders, following as it did soon after Pope Leo's open letter *Ad Anglos* in 1895, could be seen as an attempt to awaken the English to the fragility of their spiritual situation. But the wording of the letter and the terms of the decision on Anglican Orders—both heavily influenced by English Catholics not very warmly disposed to ideas of corporate reunion—more or less guaranteed that the results would be disappointing from the pope's point of view.[7] In the eyes of at least some in the Vatican, the Malines initiative might have suggested that corporate reunion was not, after all, a fantasy, and·that something like Pope Leo's hopes from two decades earlier might still be imaginable. On the Anglican side, anything that implied the possibility of a serious rethinking of the modern doctrine of the Petrine ministry as a result of Anglican arguments would have confirmed the significant role of the Anglican Church as a kind of mediating presence between East and West, consolidating the trust and respect for the Church of England shown by so many Orthodox Churches around this time. And evidence that the Roman Catholic Church was reforming itself would have strengthened the hand of those in the Church of England who were being criticized for "Romanizing," as it would imply that the movement was not all in one direction.[8]

But the painful truth was that whatever these imagined benefits, they were almost bound to be outweighed by the challenges to prevailing institutional orthodoxies. As we shall see at more length in the next chapter, the fundamental question running through the Malines discussions was one that neither party at the time had much institutional will to resolve. It was essentially the question of how Christians recognize the same faith in one another, even when polity and vocabulary are in some respects divergent. Roman Catholics were wary of any formulation that might suggest that it was possible to identify a sort of necessary minimum for such recognition, partly because this inevitably weakened the coherence of their view of ecclesiastical authority. Anglicans faced the difficulty of the apparently irreducible diversity of opinion within their Church, and the elusiveness of its decision-making processes. When Cardinal Mercier expressed his surprise and disappointment at Archbishop Davidson's reluctance to give a clear theological directive as to the desirability of this or that model of Church unity,[9] he did not fully appreciate the complexity of the archbishop's position and the lack of any specifically theological authority inhering in it (as distinct from the authority of any bishop's teaching ministry). No Anglican in the Malines group could have given a clear answer as to what process might have to be followed in order to implement any proposal for a reconciliation of ministries or any other possible practical outcome to the debates. To put it in oversimple terms, Roman Catholics were being pressed to claim *less* than they had been used to, and Anglicans were being urged to affirm *more*. The history of the reception of the ARCIC Agreed Statements shows that the difficulties raised by this have yet to be fully faced and overcome, but those statements themselves also show what may follow from at least taking seriously the methodology of much of the Malines discussions in seeking an honest picture of doctrinal history in a way not dominated by polemic or by a mere arguing for victory.

3

Issues

The Petrine Ministry

The first Conversations in 1921 evidently took time to settle on a focus for discussion, despite the acceptance of a substantial memorandum by Lord Halifax as a basis for proceeding; but there is mention early on of the Anglicans asking what it is that makes a particular truth to be *une vérité de foi* for Roman Catholics. The response enumerates three criteria—universal and explicit consent in the Church, the decision of an ecumenical council (defined as one convened or presided over by the pope), and the declaration of the pope himself speaking *ex cathedra*. This last is further clarified by Mercier's own intervention, stressing that a dogma defined by the Church corporately or the pope personally is never a "new truth" but a bringing to light of what is already *en germe* in the revelation given by Christ and the apostles. The point is to allay anxieties that the papal office has a power or charism separate from that of the Church as a whole in determining dogma, and in a slightly later exchange,[1] when the Anglican formulation of Scripture as an "ultimate standard" for a belief being regarded as *de fide* is under discussion, the Roman Catholic response claims that any dogmas defined as *de fide* are always as a matter of fact grounded in Scripture (*se réclament de l'Écriture*

Sainte). However, this is not to compromise on the threefold criteria set out earlier. Mercier goes on to argue that there is—even independently of the evidence of Scripture and Tradition—a strong *a priori* case for something like a sovereign power in the Church to counterbalance the divisive pressures that arise in a worldwide community, a unifying authority like that of the bishop in the diocese and the priest in the parish. In the exchanges that follow this intervention, both Robinson and Frere agree that a ministry of unity is required, and that this can indeed be recognized as the unique charism of the See of Rome; but that this should not be translated into terms of ecclesiastical law. The pope's insistence on his supposed canonical rights in the past has in fact been a major cause of *dis*unity in the Church. These issues recur in the record of the second Conversation, in which there is debate about the boundaries between papal jurisdiction and the ordinary jurisdiction of the diocesan bishop. Portal observes that there is some disagreement among Catholic theologians on whether the diocesan bishop's jurisdiction is *derived* from the See of Peter or merely *authorized in its exercise* by Rome. There is a rather surprising convergence between Robinson and Van Roey on the theoretical possibility of the pope retaining universal jurisdiction in theory but exercising it only in matters affecting the entire body of faithful as a way of squaring the circle here; but we must not suppose that Robinson was thereby *accepting* the premise of universal papal jurisdiction.

It was Robinson who at the third of the Conversations, set out in simple terms the ground of the Anglican objection to the developed papal system. His essay on "The Position of St. Peter in the Primitive Church"[2] was the first real "position paper" written for the Malines group, and it reflects an approach that would have been broadly recognizable to many of his Anglican contemporaries. Robinson begins with an exposition of Pauline ecclesiology drawn from the Letter to the Ephesians (a text on which he had published an authoritative commentary in 1903), pointing out that there is no hint in Ephesians of "an earthly center of unity...found in a chief of the Apostolic band."[3] Either the writer of Ephesians did not know of the Matthaean text in which Jesus declares that he will build his Church on the rock of Peter, or he did not interpret it in any way that implied a unique and lasting charism bestowed on Peter. Robinson thus discusses the New Testament references to Peter in the light of what he regards as a telling *silence* about Peter, or at least about Peter as receiving a unique gift of authority—a silence in the Pauline corpus, the Acts of the Apostles, and the Gospels themselves.[4] The text from Matthew, says Robinson, might be a compelling piece of evidence if it stood alone; but—apart from the negative evidence of the rest of Christian Scripture—Matthew's Gospel itself shows the same authority of "binding and loosing" that is bestowed on Peter being given to the whole apostolic company. The natural conclusion is surely that, even if this authority was given first to Peter, it could not have been an exclusive gift.[5] Robinson adds a summary of his conclusions, recognizing that Peter is very clearly given a "primacy of leadership" among the Twelve, but denying that this could, in the New Testament context, be understood as any sort of jurisdictional superiority, and asking in effect whether we could imagine St. Paul agreeing that St. Peter had some sort of jurisdiction over the churches to whom he (Paul) wrote his epistles. It is an indirect challenge to the notion of the pope's "ordinary" jurisdiction in every local church, perhaps the most contentious claim of the First Vatican Council in Anglican (and Orthodox) eyes.

Robinson is insistent that he is not ruling out postscriptural considerations in assessing the credibility of later papal claims, but what he believes he has shown is that biblical evidence alone will not sustain these claims. The long response from Batiffol (nearly twice the length of Robinson's paper) summarizes and replies to each of Robinson's points, but from the point of view of *method*, it seems clear that what Batiffol intends is to show that Robinson cannot be right in suggesting that the New Testament evidence is *incompatible* with the modern doctrine of the Petrine ministry. Thus, Paul may not mention Peter in Ephesians, but that is because he is preoccupied here with unity at a high level of theological abstraction—the unity between Jew and Gentile that is secured solely by the work of Christ, the unity of diverse charisms in the Body, and so on. He is not trying to address questions about the resolution of disputes in the Church. As for other passages (not dealt with by Robinson, or not adequately dealt with in Batiffol's eyes): Paul's admission in Galatians that he spent more time with Peter than with the other "pillars" of the Church in Jerusalem and his mentions of Peter in 1 Corinthians as primary witness to the resurrection must surely imply that Peter is more than one among equals in the apostolic company. Robinson's treatment of the Petrine material in Acts ignores the indications of Peter's activity in convening the community and acting in its name; the account of the "Council of Jerusalem" in Acts 15 shows Peter describing the exercise of a unique *mission* given to him by God in extending the boundaries of the Church.

Regarding the evidence of the Gospels, Batiffol accuses Robinson of being "parsimonious" in his reading of the texts: even Loisy—Batiffol takes the considerable risk of citing a figure who was by this date *persona non grata* in the Roman Catholic Church, and is careful to say that neither he nor Robinson would follow Loisy's method[6]—even Loisy grants that the Gospel narratives (including John 21) imply a special role for Peter, in that his (repentant and restored) fidelity to his calling is the foundation for the faithfulness of the rest of the apostles. The diverse traditions represented by Matthew 17, Luke 22, and John 21 point to a single tradition of Jesus conferring on Peter *la direction du troupeau chrétien* as *vicaire* of Jesus himself. And finally, on the "nonexclusive" character of the authority given to Peter in Matthew, Batiffol again cites Loisy to the effect that, while the apostolic presidents of the various Christian communities are recognized as having their own local powers, Peter's status seems to be more than this—a "personal" authority, not indeed exclusive of the other apostles but not simply a single instance of the more general charism.[7]

The reader may well feel that the honors are about equal in this exchange. Batiffol is right that Robinson does less than justice to the material in Galatians and 1 Corinthians, and that the Petrine texts in the Gospels are open to a more ambitious reading than Robinson assumes. However, Robinson *is* also surely right in questioning whether anything at all in the New Testament corresponds to a universal "superintendence" of the Church. Pauline ecclesiology is indeed typically preoccupied with broad theological concerns about the Body of Christ, but when the apostle does turn to the detail of local controversy, there is no hint that there exists any higher court of appeal. There is also another difficulty in connection with Batiffol's use of Loisy—one that he awkwardly acknowledges in passing. Loisy certainly supports a "proto-papal" reading of various Gospel texts; but he does so on the assumption that these texts are not literal records of the words of Jesus, nor even from the first generation of the Christian communities. He is a dangerous ally for Batiffol's case, as he is not interested in legitimizing papal authority based on the explicit words of Christ; what exactly the tradition of a "vicariate" of Peter rests on at the beginnings of Christianity remains entirely unclear in Loisy's scheme. Robinson might well have responded to this use of Loisy by arguing that the Modernist scholar is working with a model of an already fairly well-developed ecclesial organization in the second or third generation after Jesus as the location for the idea of Petrine supremacy; this tells us little or nothing about what Jesus or indeed Paul might have thought about Peter and leaves us still without cast-iron clarity about the roots of a theology of Petrine ministry.

The implicit weight of Robinson's argument is that there is nothing to bear out the contention that the very first Christians believed in a universal and unique authority exercised by Peter to guarantee the unity of the Church (as opposed to a loosely defined ministry of leadership and a recognition of some sort of seniority in apostolic ministry). Batiffol qualifies this in several important respects but is in danger of proving too much by way of his use of Loisy and tacitly conceding the point that the very earliest Christian generation gives us no conclusive evidence. The argument is thus already shifting toward the question that Robinson explicitly says he does not intend to address—the weight that could and should be given to postscriptural material, or, more precisely, the reading of the scriptural texts by the Fathers. This is the subject of B. J. Kidd's submission to the third Conversation, a paper that concedes that even before 400 or so, there was a strong consensus that the See of Rome alone in the West could claim an apostolic foundation (by Peter and Paul) and that its bishop held a distinctive position of "supremacy." Only during and after the pontificate of Damasus (366–84) did the claims made for this supremacy, especially in terms of the papacy as a final court of appeal, become more specific and juridical: the Matthaean commission to Peter, which had not generally been interpreted before this period as a charter for the papacy, was cited more regularly, and the claim was advanced that bishops (at least in Italy, Spain, and North Africa) derived their ministry or episcopal authority in some sense from the See of Peter.[8]

Batiffol's reply to Kidd is instructive: he freely grants that there is a history of development to be traced, and that we should not project later models backward on to the first three centuries; but he also notes the clear evidence of appeal to the Roman See from churches elsewhere from an early date. It seems that the Petrine See is recognized early on as having some sort of more-than-local responsibility for resolving problems and delivering authoritative rulings. For Batiffol, this is grounded in the fact that Christ's (Matthaean) commission to Peter is the first "episcopal" commission; thus the other apostles and the whole episcopate subsequently "insert themselves" in a succession that begins with

Peter.[9] The derivation of episcopal authority from the Roman See is thus "retrospective," not a matter of immediate contemporary dependence; nonetheless, it is a real recognition of a unique charism given to Peter and his successors, and a necessary unifying presence in virtue of being the common source of all episcopal ministry. Even Cyprian, whose work offers considerable interpretative challenges for a straightforward papalist case, seems to say something like this. Batiffol's conclusion is therefore that there is a primitive conviction that the Roman Church is the *centre de gravité* of the whole global Church, and its bishop is the "arbiter" of communion.[10]

Kidd had noted that the fifth-century language about the episcopate deriving from Peter and the See of Peter as its *auctor* is already claiming nearly everything claimed for the papacy at Vatican I, stopping short only of infallibility;[11] Batiffol agrees, commenting that "sovereignty" in matters of faith *implies* infallibility.[12] But this exchange between Anglican and Roman Catholic voices is no more straightforward than that between Batiffol and Robinson. Batiffol seems to draw back from citing or defending the full-blown language of Vatican I about universal "ordinary" jurisdiction, stressing that the derivation of episcopal from papal ministry is first and foremost a matter of *chronological succession*: the link is mediated by the history of episcopal succession across the ages, and there is no suggestion that the pope is in any sense *delegating* to another officeholder something that here and now belongs to him. While Batiffol asserts that juridical primacy involves the assumption of infallibility, he does not give any detailed argument in support of this. Apart from this reference to infallibility, Batiffol does not in fact come to any conclusions dramatically different from Kidd's, though (as in his reply to Robinson) he quite defensibly corrects and augments the Anglican argument. It would have been interesting to have his response to Kidd's further paper at this set of sessions, dealing with what aspects of papal jurisdiction were *explicitly* repudiated in the English Reformation,[13] a paper that argues that the rejection of the pope's temporal and administrative supremacy would still leave open the question of a spiritual primacy that did not involve directive authority in these spheres. In yet another paper (both Kidd and Batiffol were kept very busy at the third of the Conversations!), replying to Van Roey's essay on the theology of the episcopate's relation to the papacy, Kidd makes explicit his difficulty with any account of papal authority that in effect creates "two heads in each local church."[14] We may take it that what he sees as being rejected in the English Reformation is precisely any version of a theology of Petrine ministry that allows a presumption of papal "direct rule" in the local church, and he challenges his Roman Catholic colleagues to clarify the consistency of Vatican I with statements by Leo XIII that appear to concur with his anxieties and with historic Anglican concerns.

What emerges from the erudite and often very compressed pages of the several substantial memoranda on the Petrine ministry presented in 1925 to the third set of sessions at Malines (including the further papers by Van Roey and Hemmer) is a nuanced picture. Anglican hesitations about the direct "divine right" claim for the papacy's authority, about its scriptural foundation, and about its apparent claim to direct local jurisdiction are not brushed aside by the Roman Catholic respondents. Batiffol takes at least as sophisticated a historical approach as the Anglicans, arguably even more so (he shows more acuity about some patristic documents than does Kidd). He allows that the modern version of papal government does indeed have a *history*, and that one cannot simply read off current practice from a study of the early centuries. But he also argues strongly that a version of "Catholic" identity without the Bishop of Rome as its focus is unhistorical. Hemmer, in a magisterial survey of appeals to the papacy from the Christian East as well as the Christian West in the centuries prior to the schism of 1054,[15] makes the same case: it is impossible to deny that the Roman See is recognized throughout the

Christian world as a "supreme court," authorized to settle local disputes and rectify injustices. Hemmer distinguishes the "right of intervention" that this seems to imply[16] from the idea of the pope as the immediate source of episcopal jurisdiction in each diocese—a notion that gains popularity in some quarters in the late Middle Ages.[17] Such a theology explains much of the administrative centralization of late medieval and post-medieval Roman Catholic practice—not least in the growing claims of the papacy to control episcopal elections. Hemmer notes, however, that earlier practice has not entirely disappeared and that there is no reason why a reconciled Anglican body should not be accorded a degree of liberty in this respect, always granted that the pope has the inalienable responsibility of securing the unity of the Church and the purity of its faith regarding the process. There is, in other words, a tacit recognition among the Roman Catholic participants that both administrative centralization as a practical matter and the theological issues around the pope's status as *auctor* of episcopal ministry are legitimate matters of debate. Van Roey, like Mercier, gives a careful explanation of what papal infallibility does and does not mean; but it is interesting to note that the Anglican essays do not focus on this as a first-level question. Their concern is a more basic one: what is the rationale, what is the definition, and what are the limits of the claim to some unique and permanent charism for the papacy, such that it becomes essential for the full life of the Body of Christ on earth? The issue of infallibility is a question that can only be intelligibly discussed in the light of this more fundamental set of concerns.

In a way that does indeed foreshadow some of the work of ARCIC (and some of the work of recent Roman Catholic–Orthodox discussions of the subject), there are already signs in these exchanges of a theology of the Petrine ministry in the Church that could be ecumenically acceptable. Bracketing for a moment the question of infallibility, the essential disagreement at Malines between Anglicans and Roman Catholics might be summed up as a difference of perspective on the way in which the authority of a supreme "court of appeal" in the Church should be understood. For the Roman Catholics, recognizing the papacy as a final court of appeal entails recognizing a right of *intervention*, which to some (not wholly clear) extent also legitimizes what we might call a "preventative" authority exercised, for example, to avoid the election of unsuitable bishops. The papacy's authority may be less than a direct "ordinary" jurisdiction in every diocese, but it is more than a right of convening and arbitrating. It is properly *proactive*. The Anglican position, in contrast, assumes a more *reactive* role for the Roman See. The papacy could never have more than a constitutional sovereignty in the Church, expressed in the general recognition of its status as the proper destination of unsettled local cases but *not* involving anything that could be called the superintendence of local affairs or any right to interfere in the governance of a diocese. Such a picture would not, of course, imply that a diocese had no accountability to the wider Catholic fellowship; but this would have to work through the nests and networks of local accountability that had grown up in various regions—the synodical and metropolitical structures to which a bishop would be canonically bound. The Catholic participants at Malines are eager to insist that the right of papal intervention is not something that threatens such networks; it is only ever an extreme and exceptional measure to restore Catholic order or orthodoxy and could only be justified on the grounds that a local question was affecting the well-being or credibility of the entire Church.

The caution of the Anglicans on this subject has something to do with the history of a papacy eager to consolidate its control: Kidd draws a distinction between the right to administer a vacant see and then restore those administrative powers to their proper holder when a new bishop is appointed and the interpretation of this as process by which the local rights "revert" to the higher authority that properly holds them before being once again delegated; and he suggests that the problem with a proactive papal jurisdiction is that this distinction is increasingly eroded in the history of the Western Church.[18] The ultimate point of divergence in principle here is the Anglican unwillingness to agree that papal jurisdiction is part of the *divinely ordained* constitution of the Church, rather than a providential aid to the coherence and good order of the Body of Christ as it has actually evolved in history. As Kidd puts it,[19] the evidence of Scripture and the facts of primitive Christian history are not such that the developed claims for a *jure divino* papacy are the *only possible* extrapolation. They may be a *defensible* conclusion, and it may well be acceptable to maintain communion with those who hold such a conclusion; but it ought to be possible on this basis to grant that disagreement about the larger theological claims of the papacy should not disrupt sacramental communion. The point about the method of argument here is something we shall be returning to.

Kidd—and probably most of the Anglican group at Malines—are thus envisaging a possible unified Church in which there may be a canonical agreement about the papacy's role in settling disputes and perhaps also of coordinating acts and statements of witness relevant to the entire global Church, but without universal agreement about the charisms claimed by Vatican I. It is arguably the situation that prevailed in the first millennium, and in some respects in the first half of the second millennium also. A Roman Catholic might well object, however, that if it is possible to hold divergent views on this matter, the larger claims of Vatican I make no sense; they are universal or they are nothing. If they are no more than *possible* extrapolations from an earlier situation, they cannot reasonably be given any canonical embodiment; they are too ambitious to be merely local arrangements. This is not an argument pursued at Malines, nor particularly in more recent debate, but it is a point worth considering. Is it the case that a united Church recognizing the authority of the See of Rome as a court of appeal, but *not* acknowledging any kind of ordinary jurisdiction or any charism of delivering *irreformable* judgments would have to repudiate the conclusions of Vatican I? Or is it in fact the case that Vatican I *is* the only possible conclusion to be drawn from the data of primitive Christianity? And how could this be authoritatively established, given that a verdict on the issue that depended on papal authority would beg the question?

The Limits of Doctrinal Affirmation

It is just this issue of what kind of limited divergences in belief could be tolerated in a united Church that comes to the fore in the fourth set of Conversations. Bishop Gore's paper *On Unity with Diversity* was not included with the other papers submitted at Malines in the 1930 collection edited by Halifax, for reasons that are far from clear, although Batiffol's response to it was printed. It was not available in print until 1935,[20] but it expressed more fully than any other contribution to the discussions the heart of the Anglican problem and made explicit the hesitations felt about the method of doctrinal definition that seemed to have prevailed in modern Roman Catholic practice. Gore began with Cyprian's opinion, quoted by Augustine, that *diversum sentire,* "thinking differently" on certain subjects, was acceptable in the Church, always granted a fundamental set of conditions for communion. As Batiffol sums it up in his response, Cyprian recognized that there were differences or errors that did not make those who held them heretics.[21] Where then do we find the conditions that are necessary for communion? For Gore, this must be in some version of the "Vincentian canon"—what has been believed "everywhere, always and by everyone"; in essence, this means the doctrines of the Catholic Creeds, but none of those doctrines that have been elaborated in subsequent centuries as possible implications of those fundamentals—particularly transubstantiation, the medieval teaching on purgatory, infallibility, and the Immaculate Conception of Mary. Gore makes a distinction between doctrines resting on strong and primitive evidence and those arrived at by some sort of *inference* from the former. Surely the latter cannot claim to be believed with the same level of security without fundamentally altering what we mean by "faith" itself?

Gore's aim is not to argue against such doctrines in themselves, but to ask about the grounds on which they could be advanced as necessary conditions for ecclesial communion. Rather like Kidd in his approach to the developed modern theology of the Petrine ministry, he can envisage a future Church in which certain doctrines might be regarded as possible or defensible extrapolations from the more central items of faith but not proposed as a condition of sacramental unity. Batiffol's reply—as careful and sophisticated as his responses to Robinson and Kidd—takes two lines of argument, one perhaps rather stronger than the other. The obvious point has first to be made, that the developed conciliar theology of the person of Christ involves a great deal of inference from more basic affirmations but is nonetheless surely part of what would need to be accepted as a basic condition for unity; as Batiffol observes,[22] Newman (much quoted in this essay) can grant that pre-Nicene theology is on the surface as compatible with Arianism as with Nicene orthodoxy—perhaps indeed more so. A literal application of the Vincentian rule would have no way of dealing with this and so would leave us with a much-impoverished trinitarian and christological theology. Newman's scheme presupposes that any new statement of doctrine is an articulation not necessarily of what is formally implied but of what is "virtually" contained in the complex of language, practice, and discipline that constitutes primitive Christianity;[23] as such, it needs no alien stimulus to draw it out (this was Loisy's mistake and that of other Modernists, says Batiffol), as it is simply the organic growth of a system over time. But this means, second, that there must be some mechanism within the Church that *sanctions* certain inferences. Thus, we may believe in the virginal conception of Christ based on the scriptural witness, and in the sinless conception of the Mother of God because the Church assures us that this is a proper implication—even if not a formal or logical one—of the basic christological truths to which we assent. There is no difference in the truth of the two propositions and so no difference in the claim they make on our adherence; the difference is only in the "criteria" by which we judge them to be true.

This second point is more problematic than it initially appears. The belief that the Church's discernment in sanctioning new elaborations of belief is embodied in the Bishop of Rome is itself, as we have seen, an inference capable of challenge; and the definition of the Immaculate Conception as *de fide*, to be believed with the same certainty as the doctrines of the Creeds, does directly raise the question of the papal authority to make definitive proclamations of the limits of orthodoxy, as this definition is unmistakably one that depends on accepting this claim for the Roman See (the same could also now, of course, be said of the 1950 definition of the assumption of the Mother of God). There is a risk of circularity. But there is a more basic question that Batiffol does not address. He alludes[24] to the remark of de Maistre that belief would be more "angelic" if it had never been obliged to define and develop; as he says, de Maistre had some influence on Newman's understanding of development, and the early Newman certainly thought of doctrinal definition as a regrettable necessity.[25] Batiffol responds robustly to this, saying that it underrates the benefit of a deeper intellectual penetration of revealed mysteries. But that is not quite the point. What de Maistre and the young Newman are saying is *not* that revelation should not be explored with the intellect, but that the *definition* of its precise implications is a mixed blessing. The question ought to be, surely, what it is that makes a definition *necessary*. Batiffol does not help us here, and, in fairness, Gore does not provide us with much guidance either, as his Vincentian model is awkwardly close to the somewhat static picture of orthodoxy that Newman was reacting against in the Anglican theology of his day. It may be that to illuminate this we need to go back to our earlier distinction between proactive and reactive models of papal authority and make the point more general. Does the definition of doctrine happen simply as an organic outgrowth of the Church's self-understanding or as a response to the sort of crisis that endangers the fundamental integrity of faith?

Historically speaking, it is difficult to deny that the history of the formulation of dogma in the early Church is a history of attempts to rule out unacceptable or inadequate versions of teaching about God and Christ, rather than a record of the progressive unfolding of the implications of primary data. In other words, it is essentially reactive. The shape of the arguments around these formulations is consistently that such and such a form of words will distort or reduce the full meaning of the revelation given in Christ. Hence the regular appeal in patristic discussion to the implications of certain theological ideas for the understanding of salvation in general and the sacramental life of the Church in particular. It is not in any way a prohibition or demeaning of intellectual enquiry, but it picks up specific styles and conclusions in theology with a view to asking whether they do justice to what needs to be said about Christ if the common life of Christians is to make sense. To put it a little more specifically, if the heart of Christian distinctiveness is in the belief that through baptism Christians come to share in the relation that the eternal Logos has with the eternal Source of all, the relation of the Son to the Father in the Trinity, it should be impossible to use language that denies the Son's full share in divine life, or the completeness of humanity and divinity in the Son, or the transfiguring, "deifying" power of the Spirit in bringing about adoption in baptism and nourishing us in the Eucharist with the life of Christ's glorified humanity. The *obligation* of doctrinal definition — up to and including the immensely complicated formulations of the early Byzantine period concerning the two natures and wills of Christ (referred to by Batiffol as a clear case of inferences being pursued and defined) — is the obligation to maintain in its full clarity the character of the Christian promise and hope as regards our incorporation into the life of the Godhead. It could be said of the formulae of doctrinal definition in this period, according to their defenders, that anyone failing to draw *these* inferences from what we earlier called the "complex of language, practice, and discipline" that made up early Christianity, including Scripture and sacramental liturgy, would not have grasped what was unique about Christian faith itself.

Here is the dual difficulty for an "inference" theory of the sort Batiffol and others are advancing in the discussions at Malines: What is the crisis of doctrinal integrity that *necessitates* making explicit these matters allegedly implied in earlier formulae? And how can it be shown that the implications are such that anyone failing to accept them would demonstrably not understand what those earlier formulae truly meant? Gore's paper was asking a perfectly proper question but failing to spell out quite what made fundamental doctrines so fundamental. Batiffol is right to make the point he makes about how this is not to restrict doctrinal development to matters of formal or logical entailment, but he fails in showing why certain pieces of "virtual," informal implication need to be spelled out as necessary for the affirmation of the prior doctrines. If a is the square root of b, then to deny the proposition that b equals a squared means that you have not understood what a square root is. That is a clear case of formal and necessary implication. Now relatively little doctrinal formulation has quite that character; but we could take the example of the denial that Christ had a created human mind and will, and show that to deny this would leave us with an incoherent account of what it means for the incarnate Christ to restore every aspect of human nature. It would not be a matter of showing that there

44

were strict verbal contradictions involved, only of demonstrating that the denial would make a number of aspects of Christian behavior and speech significantly less intelligible. So, the question that needs exploring in the case of a doctrine like transubstantiation or the Immaculate Conception of Mary is whether its denial would make unintelligible the central identifying practices of Christians, in such a way that it would be impossible to recognize that a denier of the doctrine truly shared one's own belief in the incarnation.

Newman's great essay on development argued that the medieval doctrine of the treasury of merits along with many other aspects of medieval and early modern devotional or theological theses should be seen as growing organically out of the way baptism was doctrinally understood.[26] It is a bold and creative response to the standard polemical view of these later doctrines, and the case is made very largely by appealing to pastoral pressure and the need to articulate a coherent and compassionate approach to post-baptismal sin. In these terms, it is undoubtedly possible to see the developed doctrine as indeed a "reactive" solution to certain issues around the understanding and cultivation of Christian holiness. What is less clear is whether someone challenging that developed doctrine — or simply unaware of it — should be said *not to have understood what baptism means*; in which case both Orthodox and Reformed Christians have a defective grasp of baptism. Any determination of the doctrinal status of the teachings about merit and penance discussed by Newman that concluded that these "inferential" doctrines had to be held by anyone now claiming to be committed to a Catholic doctrine of baptism would create severe problems for any recognition of authentic Christian baptism outside the Roman Catholic Church. This has not generally been a route down which Catholic authority has wished to go, and the Augustinian recognition of valid baptism in schismatic bodies has prevailed. In fact, Newman's argument is *not* about whether this or that later doctrinal formulation must be

held as of faith, as an inseparable element in any orthodox understanding of primary revelation. It is more about the *legitimacy*
of these more elaborate formulations. He is responding to the
Reformed charge that they are distorted and arbitrary outgrowths
that undermine the plain sense of primitive faith. Newman is saying that a historical community exercising its intellect on the data
of faith in practice and the character of holy life in the Church
quite properly and naturally "follows through" the implications
of what it is saying and doing and produces fresh insight, which
in its matured form may indeed look very different from where it
all started. What he does *not* discuss is the degree to which the
Catholic body is bound, not to grant the orthodoxy or admissibil-
ity of these developments, but to insist that *they alone express the
essential content of the basic doctrine.*

One further difficulty arising in regard to the informal or
"virtual" inference that both Newman and Batiffol appeal to is
the extent to which such reasoning is conditioned by cultural and
local standards for judging what sorts of inference are congru-
ent or natural. Batiffol, as we have seen, insists that no factors
extraneous to the deposit of revelation affect the informal reasoning of the Church. What is defined in its developed form is the
result of the Church's own growing self-understanding alone, but
this is to make a very large assumption about the gap between
Christian reasoning and its cultural milieu. To take one example,
Newman speaks[27] of the evolving recognition of the Mother of
God as "a loving Mother with clients," a "Patroness or Paraclete"
for those who turn to her for aid. The process by which Mary's
intercession comes to be seen as especially or uniquely potent
is a complex and fascinating story to trace, but it is no disservice
to the cultus of the Mother of God to note that the language of
patron and client takes for granted a particular social order — not
one that derives from Christian principle and self-reflection, and
one indeed that Christian principle might well want to challenge
in many respects. To put it more generally, informal inference

is more vulnerable to the conditioning of historical and social circumstances than its defenders might want to allow, and this might suggest a certain caution about imposing the conclusions of such a process of inference on the entire Christian community throughout time and space.

These are of course questions that affect the whole subject of doctrinal formulation, and theologians like Batiffol are genuinely attempting to fend off the "Modernist" conclusion that *all* doctrinal or credal formulae are contingent and negotiable. This is why it is important to have a clear rationale for doctrinal formulation, along the lines of what it is that makes sense of the distinctive character of Christian prayer and holiness, the gift of "filial" union with the loving and contemplative action of the eternal Word. It is also why it is important to raise the question of how much it is necessary to make explicit about what a doctrinal affirmation might imply, and how much weight can be given to that explication, given the fluidity of the idea of informal inference, the cultural variations that may shape the process and the basic issue of what is needed to guarantee the basic grammar of Christian distinctiveness.

These are, directly and indirectly, the issues that Bishop Gore was raising at Malines (and that had been raised less fully by Robinson and Frere at the beginning of the process). Batiffol's reply is an impressive defense of a broadly Newmanian view, freely accepting the gap between primitive and modern formulation in a way that one would expect from a critical historian of Batiffol's stature but skirting the central problem of the difference between legitimizing certain developments and imposing them as normative. The nearest he comes to tackling the point is at the very end of his paper, where he recognizes the *repugnance* felt by the Orthodox for some more modern idioms. The Catholic Church is free to grant that detailed explanation needs to be undertaken to show what these modern formulae do and do not mean, just as in the early Church Athanasius was prepared to

47

recognize that some of those who resisted the Nicene definition did in fact share the same faith. Batiffol also notes, rather strikingly, the enthusiasm in some Anglican quarters for the Jesuit Maurice de la Taille's groundbreaking work on the Eucharist,[28] clarifying in a way fully acceptable to (some) Anglicans the meaning of eucharistic sacrifice. He concludes that "the definitions of faith do not only have to be explained, deepened, restored to their original elasticity; often they need to be completed"; thus, Vatican I's definition of papal authority also needs to be balanced by a full acknowledgment of the *iure divino* dignity of the episcopate.[29]

It is a prophetic observation, given that many at the Second Vatican Council saw themselves as providing just such a balancing or completion regarding the theology of Vatican I, but it leaves unanswered the question toward which the Anglicans at Malines were feeling their way. Is there a distinction to be made between what I have called reactive and proactive accounts of authority? The right to make a definitive statement that protects the integrity of Christian faith against substantial assault or distortion may well be a needful charism in the Church; and the Lucan language about Peter's call to strengthen his brethren when he has repented, with its echo in John 21, would fit well with the understanding of Petrine ministry in these terms. The right to declare certain doctrinal inferences to be necessary implications of credal orthodoxy and sacramental practice, without any specific threat to Christian integrity being involved is much more problematic. For Anglicans at Malines (and since), the inference to a personal infallibility for the Bishop of Rome that licenses further legitimizing of inferential development is itself an instance of a disproportionate valuation of the way informal reasoning works in the Church, and it invites both a carelessness and a dogmatism about the Church's actual history. Gore's appeal in his paper that the Roman communion should recognize critical scholarship as a gift and grace for the Church and indeed as something that the New Testament witness itself could be seen as supporting is (as we have seen) bound up with issues about the nature of Christian historical self-understanding that were very audibly in the background of the Malines enterprise from the beginning.

Some might see the Anglican suspicion of proactive papal authority as leaving the Church with no "living voice" to renew its witness and define its mission in changing circumstances; it is one of the points that Newman and his disciples were able to make with some plausibility against a dangerously archaeological view of authoritative doctrine, such as classical Anglican High Churchmen might be accused of holding. The problem, though, is that the exercise of the pope's powers as defined at Vatican I has not been in any obvious way a response to crises of Christian identity. There have been such in the last century and a half. And if one were looking for an example of new doctrinal definition in the face of a lethal distortion of Christian truth, the best instance might be one from outside the Roman Catholic Church. The Barmen Declaration of 1934 by representatives of the Protestant Churches in Germany fits very precisely the requirement of responding to a fundamental distortion of faith. Its affirmations make plain that there can be no authority exercised over the revelation of the Word of God by secular power, and no appeal to the supposed necessities of history or social development that can overrule the foundational character of the Church of God; thus, it should be obvious that racial discrimination in the Church is wholly inadmissible. As supporters of Barmen were to insist, there can be no meaningful Christian fellowship with those who justify such discrimination. To defend racial exclusivism is to show that you *do not understand the confession of Christ as Lord*. In the terms we have been using, the most basic condition for communion has been flouted, and there is an urgent need to clarify what may be a strict and formal implication of christological dogma and is at the very least a strong "virtual" ground of inference.

It would not then be wrong to see Barmen as an instance of "Petrine" clarification—reactive, but also transformative, clarifying where mission and witness must lead if the Church is not to lose its integrity. It may serve as an illustration of what kind of challenge in the contemporary setting might prompt a decisive statement of doctrinal "inference." It may also serve to make the point that a distinctively Petrine "strengthening of the brethren" by declaring the limits of doctrinal pluralism is possible in the local church and possible beyond the limits of communion with the Roman See. This is not at all to deny the rationale for a *focal* Petrine ministry with universal recognition, or to deny that the See of Rome is indeed, as the Anglicans at Malines agreed, the only plausible candidate for the exercise of such a role, on scriptural, historical, and pragmatic grounds, but it is to invite serious discussion of whether the model sanctioned by Vatican I—and foreshadowed in many medieval and early modern approaches—is adequate as a basis for this. What was challenged at Malines was both a centralized understanding of the Petrine ministry as direct *auctor* of local episcopal jurisdiction and what I have called a proactive view of papal intervention and definition. As we have seen, the Roman Catholic participants at Malines show signs of sympathy with these challenges, even when they continue to explain and defend Vatican I. Beauduin's extraordinary essay proposing a semi-independent "patriarchal" status for the See of Canterbury was based on a number of straightforwardly mistaken historical assumptions, but what it did was to invite the group to imagine a new kind of jurisdictional pattern and a new degree of liturgical and disciplinary diversity in the Western Church. Stripped of the historical fantasies around the medieval status of Canterbury, it asks, in effect, whether the plurality of a "patriarchal" structure, acknowledged in respect of the Eastern Churches, might not be a reality in the West also. Although Beauduin could not have envisaged such an extension of his argument, one obvious implication—looking at the Catholic Church as it currently exists—is that the diffused, noncentral vision he imagines for union between Rome and Canterbury might offer models for the relation of non-European churches to Rome, as the awareness of cultural diversity in the Church becomes more nuanced. Granted, the language of "patriarchates" is not likely to commend itself to a Church more conscious than ever of the gender-based inequities that have marked Christian history, but the concept of local jurisdictional units functioning with substantial independence is one that deserves more reflection, whatever the terminology.

The third and fourth of the Malines Conversations represent the most intense engagement with both historical and theological issues. The point had been made early on—by Archbishop Davidson as well as by some participants—that there had been a risk in those early stages of spending too much time on imagining what a reconciliation of ministries might entail once full doctrinal agreement had been reached, at the expense of actually dealing with what needed reconciling at the doctrinal level. Lord Halifax's original memorandum had made quite large assumptions about the extent of doctrinal convergence between the churches, for example, on the question of eucharistic sacrifice. He had appealed to the fact that Eastern and Western Christians had never disputed the validity of each other's eucharistic practice despite a significant and—apparently—irreconcilable difference as to when the "moment of consecration" occurred; could not this be a model for a new understanding of Roman Catholic–Anglican relations, and a basis for some sort of sacramental recognition as a prelude to full integration of ministries? In other words, the group at Malines was being tacitly encouraged by Halifax to concentrate on the process by which unity could be institutionally and canonically realized based on doctrinal agreement, but the participants on both sides acknowledged, once they had met, that the doctrinal convergence could not be taken for granted—or rather that there was a question about the whole understanding of doctrinal definition that had to be tackled, prior to the discussion of specific doctrinal points.

This is perhaps one of the most interesting legacies of the

Malines discussions. It is possible to talk about doctrinal divergence without raising the question of how doctrinal language itself is understood—its purpose, its rationale, and the circumstances in which it needs to be made more precise or more explicit. If it is granted that only very infrequently does a crisis arise that affects the whole Christian or Catholic body and requires decisive clarification, it is not in the least surprising or disturbing that local theologies and patterns of spirituality and liturgical style develop independently. It is important to establish what it is that continues to allow them to see in each other the same faith, so that communion can be maintained. It is less important, perhaps even counterproductive, to extend this basic set of criteria for recognition. We do not have to adopt a crude version of the Vincentian rule to define these criteria, nor do we need to deny the facts of doctrinal evolution. But to envisage the basic grammar of communion as a recognition of the grace of adoptive divine filiation as set out in Scripture and sacramental practice allows a degree of what should be manageable diversity. While it makes sense to continue to hold that the management of this diversity is precisely what constitutes the episcopal charism, this framework permits us to recognize, with the Lambeth bishops in 1920, that there are graces and gifts existing outside the communion of episcopally ordered churches that can rightly be sought by and shared with bishops in historic succession. As our discussion of the Barmen Declaration indicates, there are also circumstances in which a community separated from the historic succession can manifest in unmistakable form the true nature of the Petrine gift. In the powerful image used by Archbishop Michael Ramsey of Canterbury, evoking Martin Luther's dramatic act of protest in 1517, the Catholic Church needs to read its judgment nailed to the door in Wittenberg and be called to renewal and repentance.[30]

4

Conclusion

The abiding interest of the Malines Conversations is not simply in the way they undoubtedly set the agenda for later ecumenical discussion, particularly in the context of ARCIC. We have noted the importance of the background to the meetings in terms of the problems and preoccupations of both the Church of England and the Roman Catholic Church. It was a period in which both institutions faced the challenge of rethinking some of their historic self-understanding. Malines would not have happened had the Church of England not recovered a stronger sense of its continuity with the history and spirituality of Western Catholic Christendom; and although Halifax and his colleagues did not represent a majority in the Church of England, they did speak for a constituency that could no longer be ignored by the Church's leadership. The fact that Frere could become a bishop, although he belonged to a religious order—something whose very legality could still be questioned by convinced Protestant Anglicans—tells its own story. The vastly complicated history of Davidson's struggles over the revision of the *Book of Common Prayer* indicates both the impossibility of creating so hostile an environment in the Church of England that Anglo-Catholics would be under pressure to leave it, and the extreme difficulty of alienating a majority in the Church who were apprehensive about compromise with Roman

Catholicism. We have seen how this crisis pushed the boundaries of Anglican thinking about church-state relations. In this
context, Malines was indeed an event that, despite its small scale
and informal character, appeared to pose serious questions to the
historic Anglican establishment.

Meanwhile, in the Roman Catholic Church, the anxiety—
even paranoia—about Modernism implied an equally fundamental challenge to a historic settlement. Despite the decision of the
First Vatican Council in favor of papal infallibility, and despite
the increasingly widespread imposition of a certain style of scholastic philosophy on Catholic education and priestly formation,
Catholic theology was not as homogeneous as many wished.
More seriously, strong intellectual currents throughout the nineteenth century had favored the adoption of a more recognizable
critical method in scriptural and patristic studies. Many of those,
like Duchesne, who had moved in this direction believed that
they were helping the Church toward a more intelligent and
adequate defense of its beliefs. Newman himself, in his analysis of the nature of change in theological language and ecclesial practice, was seeking to make the Church's proclamation
less vulnerable to attack and to detach arguments for Catholic
Christianity from the defense of historically indefensible claims.
But the conclusions drawn by some, like Loisy, who were prepared to relativize the entire doctrinal system, caused concern—
understandable, but becoming rapidly bound up with a whole
set of attitudes around ecclesial loyalty and obedience. Since any
review of the Roman Catholic Church's response to Anglicanism
was bound to involve some revisionism regarding the historical
record, or an acknowledgment that some past judgments may
have been made on inadequate factual grounds, there was always
going to be a fundamental difficulty. The actual Conversations,
as we have seen, brought that difficulty into the full light of day.
Quite apart from the fact that some prominent Roman Catholic
voices at Malines had sympathies that could have been seen as

Modernist in tendency, the Conversations repeatedly returned to the question of whether Christians could recognize each other's doctrinal integrity and share communion while recognizing areas of legitimate diversity in conviction rooted in different historical experiences of mission and witness.

Both the Roman Catholic Church and the Church of England were thus being invited to take seriously the fact of historical change, to think theologically about how their positions had evolved, rather than assuming that a particular configuration of teaching and practice was of timeless validity and authority. No one at Malines would have for a moment entertained the idea that the basic shape of Christian faith should be adapted to suit intellectual or cultural fashion; the gift of grace through the Incarnate Savior, mediated in the sacramental life of a visible Church with an apostolically validated ministry, was the axiomatic starting point shared by all participants. That is perhaps where the Malines process most clearly leaves us with a contemporary agenda. What does it mean to believe in and work for a united Church that is unambiguous about its character as the embodiment of the gift of the Word Incarnate, yet is capable of translating that gift into the diverse cultural idioms of human history? The Anglican contributors to Malines ask for a recognition that this particular Christian community, while holding itself accountable to the central doctrines of the Creed, has not experienced any compelling pressure to state, let alone require belief in, certain arguable implications of those doctrines. The Roman Catholic response is to grant the reality of diversity but to stress that there must be some means of discerning between valid and invalid developments in Christian thought and practice, and that this is ultimately unthinkable without a ministry in the Church that is free to speak for the integrity of the whole Body as it seeks to respond to the challenges of the day. The modern papacy may represent a risk in some ways, given a history in which its claims have sometimes been excessively political and interventionist, but the Church as a whole has the capacity to restore balance and rectify distortions in the exercise of ministries, and this is something that Christians can pray and work for together.

Two things that come into focus here may be worth mentioning. The first takes us back to the Lambeth Appeal of 1920, which seems to have encouraged the initiative that led to Malines. The bishops write from a conviction that the episcopal ministry is a gift of God necessary for the well-being and continuance in faith of the Church, but they recognize its flawed and confused history and recognize the freedom of God in raising up effective ministries outside the episcopal succession. In so recognizing where God has bestowed gifts, they let themselves imagine a reconciliation of ministries that is genuinely reciprocal, in which they will receive from others outside the institutional succession. This prompts the question of whether a reconciliation involving the Petrine office could be thought of in any such terms: whether, without denying that this office is for the good and the continuance of the Church's faith, there could be an acknowledgment that the history of this ministry was flawed and compromised, that God has endowed communities not in communion with the See of Rome with spiritual gifts that were given for the good of the whole Body, and that there might properly be a way in which the pope could symbolically "receive" these graces in some sort of reciprocal action.

As the early stages of the Malines process show, thinking about such matters should not distract us from looking for full and robust doctrinal agreement, which in this context also means agreement about the *scope* of what is to be agreed. We have seen in this survey of some of the arguments at Malines that it is not very helpful to argue about doctrinal definition unless there is a clear sense of how and why such definition matters; and this probably means some critical thinking about any model of doctrinal development that is simply about extrapolating and authorizing inferences from the central doctrines, whether or not there is an immediate threat to Christian integrity or coherence. However, for this clear sense to be a reality, the Church needs to find a renewed understanding of what *doctrine* itself means. The Church's teaching—if we begin from the biblical model—is a matter of spelling out what we need to know in order to live consistently as members of the Body of the glorified Christ. Thus, it is important to be clear about what sorts of behavior are at odds with the reality of Christ's Body, and to be clear about what must be true of Jesus in history and of God the Holy Trinity in eternity if our lives are to make sense. To say less than the truth about the union of divine and human in Jesus is to *promise* less than Christ offers, to reduce the hope of radical transformation for human nature through the Holy Spirit. To say less than the truth about God's threefold being is to weaken the Christian hope for a share in the limitless intimacy and love that is given and received within the life of the divine persons. To say less than the truth about the sacraments of baptism and Eucharist is to reduce these moments of divinely active transformation to signs or reminders that depend on our human action and intelligence. Doctrine is whatever preserves affirmations like these from being trivialized or bent out of shape, reduced, and relativized. These are the affirmations that tell us who we are as Christians, and without them we lose our identity—and thus also lose the true depth of our communion with each other.

Doctrine is always in the service of this communion, with God and with each other. When teachings arise in the Church that jeopardize the very foundations of communion, there is a need for doctrinal boundaries to be clarified. This may mean, as in the early Church, refining the terminology used to speak about Christ so that ambiguities are ruled out; it may mean, as in medieval Byzantium, clarifying that the grace received in prayer is no less than the uncreated presence and light of the Godhead; or it may mean, as suggested earlier, the uncompromising refusal of a pseudo-theology that sanctifies anti-Christian tyranny and racial oppression, as in the Barmen Declaration, or the Kairos Document issued in South Africa in 1985. In their various ways, all such moments of definition are attempts not so much to guard a static content of belief but *to preserve the fullness of what is opened up in Christ to a redeemed humanity*. In this sense, doctrinal fidelity and theological precision are not luxuries for the churches of God.

So, too, it is not a luxury for the churches of God to have a ministry commissioned to exercise watchfulness and authority, to be free to name and rule out versions of the Christian gospel that are less than they should be. That ministry of recalling the Church to its own full integrity and identity is to a significant extent shared by the entire communion of the faithful but is embodied specially in those upon whom the Spirit is invoked in ordination. As the company of ordained minsters is one in which different levels of responsibility are assigned, we can see the episcopal ministry as concentrating this calling in an intensified way as part of the bishop's care for unity and communion in their fullness. That the worldwide fellowship of bishops itself needs a ministry of discernment and unification follows naturally: the Petrine calling to turn afresh to Christ and convert and strengthen the brothers and sisters is indeed given to the apostolic ministry as a whole, but it is very particularly present in the historic See that derives from the first apostle to receive the promise and vocation.

A Church without this ministry is a Church impoverished and potentially frustrated. Thus far, all those who shared in the Malines Conversations would probably have agreed, but the unresolved question remains. For the Anglicans at Malines, the way in which the Petrine ministry had been increasingly understood and exercised had meant that the vehicle of this ministry was becoming a hindrance to unity, not a means toward it. To put it more starkly than they themselves would have done, it is as if the Roman Catholic Church in the post–Vatican I era itself lacked a true Petrine ministry—because of the exaggerated form taken by its claims—as much as those outside the communion of the See of

Rome. For these critics, the restoration of a true Petrine ministry would entail a more critical view of how doctrinal development might be understood. Both then and (doubtless) now, the Roman Catholic response might be to say that it is eccentric and dangerous to refuse the communion of the See of Rome here and now on the grounds of historic anomalies or imbalances: The Church we live in is the Church we have to live in, and we cannot postpone our faithfulness or obedience in the Church until our conditions have been met. Refusal of this sort can lead to a kind of Gnostic perfectionism, which is once again inimical to communion in the Incarnate Word. However, both the Anglican critic and the Roman Catholic apologist might concur at least in a concern that discussion about the Petrine ministry should not become a debate over what was *required* for the recognition of orthodox belief, rather than an exploration of how a gift given to the whole Church for the sake of its integrity might be released for its fullest effectiveness.

So the discussions at Malines bring us finally back to the question of how the *wholeness* of the Church is to be understood, recognized, and nurtured. The participants in the Malines Conversations clearly did not think that there would be a simple institutional answer to this. All of them were willing, however, to move beyond the comfort zones of their institutions to consider what sort of answer there might be. In searching for a way forward, they cautiously but unmistakably sought to prompt their own ecclesial communions to reflect on the complexities of their respective histories and on some of the ways their histories threatened to imprison them. Beauduin's paper may not have been a model of historical accuracy, but it grew out of the author's life-long project of anchoring ecclesiology in a Christ-centered liturgical theology. The Anglican discussants shared the conviction that the Church of England needed to grow beyond its historic identity as the national Church and to recover its theological self-confidence and its sacramental center. The Roman Catholic members shared the conviction that a centralized system of theological control obscured the proper diversity and intellectual creativity of Christian communities. They would almost certainly also have shared the conviction, in the wake of the anti-Modernist fevers of the preceding decade, that such a system lent itself readily to abuse.

A good ecumenical dialogue cannot be about winning and losing, and part of the imaginative novelty of Malines lay in the fact that Halifax and Portal refused to think in such terms — and largely persuaded their fellow-member not to do so either. But this implies that a good ecumenical dialogue will also motivate participants to ask themselves what they might need to *receive* from those they are speaking with — and so to recognize what is in fact something fundamental to the biblical vision of the Body of Christ: the need to acknowledge our need of one another to complete our discipleship, our service, and our witness. Ecumenical discussion has advanced immeasurably since the third decade of the twentieth century, but if it is to advance further, and to lead ultimately to adequate theological agreement and sacramental reconciliation, it will need to continue to take to heart this growth into receptivity. It is common now to speak about "receptive ecumenism" — the encounter that shows our willingness to learn and to be "completed" by each other — but it is never enough to think of this only in terms of a kind of interior spiritual nourishment. The Lambeth Appeal pointed to something more, something perhaps more than its authors fully realized, and the discussants at Malines did their best to imagine what that "more" might look like. The lasting importance of the Conversations is surely in this readiness to *imagine* — certainly on the foundation of a full and unambiguous recognition of God's revelation in Christ and with a sharp and critical eye to both history and theology, but nonetheless a willingness to think that the Church is still discovering by the grace of the Spirit how to be what it truly is. In that discovery, all Christians must learn how to listen and receive.

Conclusion

Cardinal Mercier on his deathbed gave Halifax leave to publish his last letter to Archbishop Davidson if the latter approved. It is a deeply moving document, bearing ample witness to the spiritual greatness of its author. The dying cardinal states clearly that both the impatient longing for a solution (as if to a "theorem of geometry," he says), and an "all or nothing" attitude from those who are wholly preoccupied with the difficulties and can only think in terms of victory and defeat are evidence of a mind-set that fails to see the work as ultimately dependent on grace. "We set to work," the cardinal writes, "without knowing either when or how this union hoped for by Christ could be realized, but convinced that it could be realized since Christ willed it, and that we had, therefore, each one of us, to bring our contribution to its realization. Reunion is not our work, and we may be unable to achieve it, but it is within our power, and consequently within our duty, to prepare it, and *pave the way* for it."[1] It is, he continues, "in this light of apostleship" that he has engaged in the Conversations, mindful of Paul in 1 Corinthians 3:7: "neither the one who plants nor the one who waters is anything, but only God who gives the growth." That appeal to an apostolic vocation and its outworking in the shared prayer and friendship of the Malines encounters show something of the radical spirit of hope and charity that animated those who kept faith with one another in the often-challenging years of the Conversations. That spirit continues to be at the heart of all encounters that seek the restoration of the integrity of the Church's witness in our own times.

Notes

1. Introduction

1. Although the Flemish "Mechelen" is the common usage today, all the documents of the time use the French form, and I have followed this throughout.

2. Walter Frere, *Recollections of Malines* (London: Centenary Press, 1935), is a significant personal memoir. *Notes on the Conversations at Malines 1921–1925: Points of Agreement* by Viscount Halifax (Charles Lindley Wood) (London and Oxford: A. R. Mowbray, 1928), is a personal reflection by one of the main architects of the project. The bilingual publication *The Conversations at Malines 1921–1925/Les Conversations de Malines 1921–1925* (Oxford: Oxford University Press, 1927), is the official report to the archbishop of Canterbury agreed to by the Anglican participants and contains summaries of the papers presented and the group discussions. Lord Halifax published in 1930 an unauthorized compendium of most of the papers (in English and French) and a fuller set of minutes of the discussions, which—confusingly—has the same title as the official report of 1927, *The Conversations at Malines/Les Conversations de Malines 1921–1925* (London: Philip Allan, 1930). There are two thorough and reliable modern studies: John A. Dick, *The Malines Conversations Revisited* (Leuven: University of Leuven Press, 1989), and Bernard Barlow, *"A Brother Knocking at the Door": The Malines*

Conversations 1921–1925 (Norwich: Canterbury Press, 1996). The major biography of Dom Lambert Beauduin, *Un pionnier. Dom Lambert Beauduin (1873–1960): Liturgie et unite des chrétiens* by Raymond Loonbeek and Jacques Mortiau (Louvain-la-Neuve: Éditions de Chevetogne, 2001), has an excellent chapter on Malines in vol. 1, 449–530.

3. Portal was an important intellectual and spiritual influence on several French Catholic scholars whose work contributed to the theological renaissance of the period after the Second World War, and eventually to the agenda of Vatican II, including Jean Guitton and Yves Congar.

4. Anselm Bolton, *A Catholic Memorial of Lord Halifax and Cardinal Mercier* (London: Williams and Norgate, 1935), provides in chap. 3 a fascinating—though idiosyncratically personal—overview of the story. He notes that, thanks to Halifax's private initiative, two prominent Anglo-Catholic scholars, T. A. Lacey and Fr. Frederick Puller, of the well-known Anglican religious community in Oxford, the Society of St. John the Evangelist, were invited to Rome for informal consultations with the group reviewing Anglican Orders.

5. George Bell, *Randall Davidson, Archbishop of Canterbury* (Oxford: Oxford University Press, 1935), is a magisterial treatment of Davidson's life and work. On relations with the Eastern Churches, see especially chaps. 52, 58, 67–69, and 75. Chapter 79 deals fully with the Malines Conversations, reproducing much important correspondence.

6. Bell, *Randall Davidson*, 177–78.

7. The text of the Lambeth Appeal is included in Halifax's 1930 collection of materials (henceforth cited as Halifax 1930); the quotation is from p. 69.

8. Halifax 1930, 69.

9. Herbert Hensley Henson, *Retrospect of an Unimportant Life*, vol. 2 (Oxford: Oxford University Press, 1943), 137.

The chapter from which this is quoted (137–50) fully documents Henson's hostile responses to the Malines meetings.

10. Loonbeek and Mortiau, *Un pionnier*, 454–56, summarizes Mercier's troubles regarding his American visit.

11. Henson, *Retrospect*, vol. 2, 139.

12. T. F. Taylor, *J. Armitage Robinson: Eccentric, Scholar and Churchman, 1858–1933* (Cambridge: James Clarke and Co., 1991), offers a balanced and comprehensive picture of Robinson's theology. For his involvement at Malines, see 86–100. This chapter contains valuable extracts from Robinson's journal and relates his views on the Petrine ministry to the work of ARCIC. On his Eucharistic theology, see, e.g., 82–83, 84–85.

13. For the full story of Mercier's approach to Beauduin and the composition of this paper, see Loonbeek and Mortiau, *Un pionnier*, 468–71, 479–81; on the reception of Beauduin's text, 490–98.

2. Context

1. For a recent study, see T. A. Howard, *The Pope and the Professor: Pius IX, Ignaz von Döllinger, and the Quandary of the Modern Age* (Oxford: Oxford University Press, 2017).

2. See most recently an excellent study by Keith Beaumont, "The Reception of Newman in France at the Time of the Modernist Crisis," in *Receptions of Newman*, ed. Frederick D. Aquino and Benjamin J. King (Oxford: Oxford University Press, 2015), 156–76.

3. See Anselm Bolton, *A Catholic Memorial of Lord Halifax and Cardinal Mercier* (London: Williams and Norgate, 1935), 88–90.

4. George Bell, *Randall Davidson, Archbishop of Canterbury* (Oxford: Oxford University Press, 1935), 1355–56; the whole of chap. 82 gives a full account of the last stages of the controversy.

5. To the surprise of many, Bishop Henson of Durham was sufficiently dismayed by the rejection of the revised Prayer Book that he became an advocate of disestablishment; see *Retrospect of an Unimportant Life*, vol. 2 (Oxford: Oxford University Press, 1943), chap. 15, for his running commentary on the crisis.

6. See Bernard Barlow, *"A Brother Knocking at the Door": The Malines Conversations 1921–1925* (Norwich: Canterbury Press, 1996), 33–34.

7. Bolton, *Catholic Memorial*, 70–75, for some of the debate around the framing of the letter *ad Anglos*.

8. On the hopes of Anglicans to facilitate reconciliation between Rome and the Eastern Churches, see the report to the archbishop of Canterbury, *The Conversations at Malines 1921–1925/Les Conversations de Malines 1921–1925* (Oxford: Oxford University Press, 1927), 12–13. On the earlier background to Anglican initiatives in ecumenical conversation aimed at a reformed global Catholicism, see the important monograph by Mark Chapman, *The Fantasy of Reunion: Anglicans, Catholics, and Ecumenism, 1833–1882* (Oxford: Oxford University Press, 2014).

9. Bell, *Randall Davidson*, 1267–77, reproduces much of the relevant correspondence among Davidson, Mercier, and Halifax.

3. Issues

1. Halifax 1930, 18–19.

2. Halifax 1930, 89–102.

3. Halifax 1930, 90.

4. As well as 1 Peter, where one might expect some allusion to any clear tradition about primacy.

5. Halifax 1930, 100.

6. Halifax 1930, 117.

7. Halifax 1930, 121.

8. Halifax 1930, 126–28 on patristic evidence after the time of Pope Damasus, and 127–32 on earlier interpretations of the Matthaean text. For the first appearances of the idea of Peter as *auctor* of the powers of other bishops, see 127–28.

9. Halifax 1930, 143.

10. Halifax 1930, 149.

11. Halifax 1930, 128.

12. Halifax 1930, 140.

13. Halifax 1930, 151–58.

14. Halifax 1930, 183.

15. Halifax 1930, 187–240.

16. Halifax 1930, 212.

17. Halifax 1930, 223–24.

18. Halifax 1930, 180—Atzberger/Scheeben. Cf. visitatorial rights.

19. Halifax 1930, 182.

20. When it was published in Frere's *Recollections*.

21. Halifax 1930, 264.

22. Halifax 1930, 282.

23. Halifax 1930, 277.

24. Halifax 1930, 286.

25. On this, see R. Williams, "Newman's *Arians* and the Question of Method in Doctrinal History," in *Newman after a Hundred Years*, ed. Ian Ker and Alan G. Hill (Oxford: Oxford University Press, 1990), 263–85.

26. See John Henry Newman, *An Essay on the Development of Christian Doctrine: The Edition of 1845*, ed. with an introduction by J. M. Cameron (Harmondsworth: Penguin Books, 1974), 412–27.

27. Halifax 1930, 392.

28. De la Taille's *Mysterium Fidei* (Paris: Beauchesne, 1921) had already aroused a good deal of controversy in Catholic circles because of its challenge to the idea that the Mass was

an actual event of "immolation" (sacrificial slaughter). The work had indeed been well received by Anglicans (and would continue to be influential for Anglo-Catholic theologians through the twentieth century), and it was welcomed by Beauduin and other liturgiologists.

29. Halifax 1930, 285–86.

30. Michael Ramsey, *The Gospel and the Catholic Church* (London: Longmans, Green and Company, 1936), 180: "Catholicism always stands before the church door at Wittenberg to read the truth by which she is created and by which also she is judged."

4. Conclusion

1. Charles Lindley Wood (Viscount Halifax), *Notes on the Conversations at Malines 1921–1925: Points of Agreement* (London and Oxford: A. R. Mowbray, 1928), 13–14.